Spirit is talking to *You*

True Stories of Signs, Wonders,
Inspiration, Love and Connection

Compiled & Written by
Joan Doyle

CCB Publishing
British Columbia, Canada

Spirit is Talking to You:
True Stories of Signs, Wonders, Inspiration, Love and Connection

Copyright ©2012 by Joan Doyle
ISBN-13 978-1-77143-000-5
First Edition

Library and Archives Canada Cataloguing in Publication
Doyle, Joan, 1962-
Spirit is talking to you : true stories of signs, wonders, inspiration, love and connection
/ compiled and written by Joan Doyle.
ISBN 978-1-77143-000-5
Also available in electronic format.
Additional cataloguing data available from Library and Archives Canada

Cover artwork by: Joan Doyle

HOW COULD ANYONE
Words and music by Libby Roderick © Libby Roderick Music 1988.
Used by permission. From the recordings "How Could Anyone" and
"If You See a Dream" Turtle Island Records, Anchorage, Alaska
www.libbyroderick.com libbyroderick@gmail.com 907-278-6817

Sufi Dancing description used by permission of Mary Brenda McQueen.
Quote from Joe Seoane used by kind permission,
EntertainmentIndustryMinistry.org
Core Concepts of Science of Mind, used by kind permission of Centers for
Spiritual Living, Colorado.

Publisher: CCB Publishing
              British Columbia, Canada
              www.ccbpublishing.com

Praise for *Spirit is Talking to You*

"Thought provoking and uplifting, the variety of experiences described in Joan Doyle's story collection are evidence of love in action in this interconnected world that we live in. Thoroughly enjoyable."

Dr. Mark Vierra
Minister NCHRS, A United Center for Spiritual Living

"These anecdotes of love and connection will bring to mind ones own amazing and miraculous stories. It'll have you saying, "Yep, that happened to me," or "Absolutely, right on." Don't miss out on this delightful and deeply comforting read, it's one you'll want to share with friends."

Steve Rambo
Ministerial Candidate
Holmes Institute: School of Consciousness Studies

"Joan Doyle's book, "Spirit Talking to You" reveals the voice of wisdom within us all. Often drowned out by self doubt or our inner critic, this book testifies to the importance of turning up the volume on that wisdom and trusting it so that we can live fearlessly and feel more fully alive."

Beatrice Elliott
Author of *Change Your Story, Change Your Life*

"What a beautiful and inspiring collection of heartfelt experiences. Every single story either brought a tear to my eye or gave me a warm fuzzy feeling! If you are ready to read some life changing, inspiring stories, if you are ready to learn from others' experiences and make sustainable changes in your own life, don't wait, read on!!"

Patricia Missakian
Money, Branding and Marketing Coach
www.thebrandinggoddess.com

"Read on and discover a world of spiritual adventure."

Rev. Barbara Lee
Church of Truth, Center for Awakening Consciousness

To my parents John and Jane Doyle
In gratitude for your unconditional and eternal love

To my husband Justin Elledge
Thank you for your vision, love and light
And for sharing them with me.

Contributing Authors

I would like to acknowledge individual authors for permission to print the following material contained in this book.

Amanda Sargenti
Amy Lloyd
Arthur Barrett
Barbara Schiffman
Carrie McConkey-Herrera
Christy Shelton
Chrystine Julian
Dean Regan
Dearbhla Egan
Gertrude Anne Doyle
Kristina Keefer
Jon Lopez
Joseph Doyle
Julie Penman Livesey
Justin Elledge
Laurie St. Clare
Mary Hylan
Robert Duffy
Sabrina Johnson
Sandra Maclean
Sandi Duncan
Sandra Phillips
Sean M. Kelly
S. Kay
Tom Rebold

Information about the contributing authors is included at the end of this book. I would like to thank each of them for adding their colorful experiences to the rainbow expression of the deep and abiding love that created and inspires us all.

A special thanks goes to Mary Hylan, to Dr. Mark Vierra, the beautiful core of Practitioners at North Hollywood Church of Religious Science and my grammar teacher, Sr. Claude!

Table of Contents

Spirit is at work in the world today.

Spirit is at work in my world today.

Spirit is at work in me today.

The storms of the world swirl gently around me.

I am safe and secure always.

Amen!

Joseph Seoane

Introduction - A Friendly Universe

You are the spiritual light that cannot fail.
- Emma Curtis Hopkins

As a licensed spiritual counselor, I often get a quizzical response on the rare occasion I choose to explain what I do, when meeting a stranger at a party. "Oh," one person commented, "I guess Oprah made Spirit popular!" It amuses and saddens me as I acknowledge that despite the proliferation of religions in the world, our everyday reality is most often kept separate from what is considered sacred. It seems the pendulum has swung from blind faith to scientific thinking. To think that logic and rational thought are preferable to religious beliefs is very understandable when we look at the violence that has and still does result from religious fanaticism. But there is a middle ground.

Between measurable facts and organized religion is a very real living Spirit. We recognize this as a force that expresses itself diversely and to varying degrees through each and every living thing. When I speak of my ninety one-year-old mother, I say her spirit is strong even as her body is failing. Spirit is the life force unchanged, despite age or infirmity. Spirit essence can never be lost, damaged, diminished or destroyed. Inventiveness, hope, joy, love, abundance and creativity are to name but a few of its enduring qualities. What Spirit is, we are. Spirit is expansive, but given our free will we have the freedom to constrict its expression through us or to allow it to flow freely and enhance our life experience.

We know we are in the flow of this living Spirit when we feel generous and enthusiastic, or we feel centered and at peace. We sense all manner of possibilities. We also know when we are

1

hindering this source energy if we feel stuck, fearful, critical, resentful or angry.

Available equally to all, Spirit is used differently by each according to his/her beliefs. One person believes the only way he can have wealth is to steal: his view of life is one of scarcity and lack. Another believes she can be wealthy by putting her heart and soul into her work, and she puts love into every math lesson she teaches. Her world is one of satisfaction and purpose. Beliefs have the power to shape our individual realities.

So what about when bad things happen? It is my belief that nothing that happens in our lives is a mistake. We may view events negatively or as disruptions to how we imagined our lives should be progressing, but from the perspective of the soul, things look very different. Unwelcome events can cause us to seek answers, to soul search. It is never a mistake to seek to know who we truly are, who we have always been and always will be, beyond the vehicle of the body. We seek to know what is most real about us.

Mother Teresa saw from the perspective of soul: beyond appearances, beyond ideas of earned value, beyond judgment. In Spirit we are all precious and deserving. In Spirit we are magnificent, whole, and perfect as we are and where we are. If we have work to do, it is to cut away all that says otherwise in our own minds. The beliefs we consciously and unconsciously accept and nurture in a world focused on achievement, wealth, comparison and materialism have limited our ideas of ourselves.

If we can accept the constancy of change in the external circumstances of our lives and sit quietly as the witness, the detached observer, we move closer to communing with the presence of the changeless within us. The moment we choose to do this— not resisting the less pleasant aspects of life and even the mundane everyday chores—it transforms our experience. Allowing things to be as they are, the struggle ceases and we find peace: peace with our lives, with ourselves and peace with the world. *Being in the world but not of it*, we are now a clearer channel for the Spirit to express itself and to do through us what is ours to do.

So if we are open to it, we can hear Spirit talking to us through every stick and stone and creature, every person, circumstance or task. It is talking to us of wisdom when the trees shed their leaves to survive the cold of winter. Our good friends confirm that we are supported and loved, and make it easy for us to be our best selves. Difficult relationships ask us to grow in love, patience, and understanding. The dawn is Spirit's reassurance of hope, and the sunset its blanket of rest. Our world is a daily miracle and so are we.

Albert Einstein believed that the most important choice we will ever make is whether we live in a friendly universe or not. The majority of the contributors to this book believe in a supportive, wise presence as the source of all life and that it is always available for conversation, willing to comfort and guide. Inviting the wisdom of Spirit into their living room, their car, their workplace, the belief is, *wherever I am, God is.* And God, or the Living Spirit, is always an aspect of love. Their faith is constant, active and real, not just practiced inside a church, mosque, or synagogue on a given day. It is not limited by the way the world thinks. It is a connection in consciousness that some choose not to define. In every case it is something personal and mysterious and sacred.

As you read, listen and soften as Spirit speaks to you through these very pages.

I hope whatever your chosen path that you know that you are unique, precious and loved, that you are more powerful than you know, and that you are never alone. You are here for a reason and the world is a better place for it.

The Spirit in me recognizes the Spirit in you,
Joan Doyle

Signs

*A little consideration of what takes place around us every day
would show us that a higher law than that of our will regulates events…
our painful labors are unnecessary and fruitless….only in our easy,
simple spontaneous action are we strong.*
- Emerson

Signposts from Spirit or your Higher Self take many and varied forms. Pennies that say, "In God We Trust" are symbols for many, even if it just means good luck. White feathers for some symbolize an angel visitation, meaning they are being protected or comforted; they are not alone. Playing cards found on the street each have a meaning in Tarot, and are messages for some who believe in it. Your symbols are unique to you.

If you wish guidance in this way and you don't have a symbol that you have recognized or decided to believe is yours yet, I encourage you to ask for one. Stay open and watchful to the events of your day and your responses to them. Watch how you feel when you see what you think is your sign. It will break your train of thought so you can either shift your thinking or affirm that you are on the right track. You attribute meaning to your sign depending on the events and thoughts surrounding it. Don't over think it. Take a playful attitude and let yourself be guided by a feeling of peace and comfort. You will see your signs when you least expect it.

See A Penny

By Justin Elledge

"See a penny, pick it up,
All the day, you'll have good luck!"

We have often heard this about pennies found on the sidewalk - that it's good luck, a sign of the abundance of the universe or gifts from angels.

I developed a slightly different twist on the found penny after a friend told me how empowered he felt whenever he found a coin on the path.

Larry was like a mentor to me. A former navy pilot in WWII, parent, grandfather and "uncle" to many, he was a man of few words. When he spoke he always seemed to be able to bring life into focus and explain what was really important; what really mattered in our day to day lives.

One day, we were walking towards a restaurant, when we both spotted a shiny penny on the sidewalk that someone had dropped. He turned to me and said, "This must be my lucky day, my prayer answered!"

"You are lucky," I said "but it is only a penny."

"Only a penny? Only a penny?" he exclaimed and over lunch he went on to explain to me how much more than a penny it was.

At that time in my own life, I was working really hard and try as I might, I never quite felt like I was getting ahead. No matter what I did it always seemed like something would come along and upset the apple cart. I told this to Larry and he asked me, "Do you pray Justin?"

And I said "Every Sunday" And we both laughed. Then he asked another question, "How often do you listen?"

"What do you mean?" I replied inquisitively. He went on. "You say you pray one day a week, but how many days a week do you listen?"

"I don't understand."

"You know what it is to pray, you are asking for help from the almighty. My question is, how often does the Almighty reply?"

Somewhat sheepishly I answered, "I don't know that I ever listened, I figured if God was listening and answered my prayer, he would definitely let me know."

"You mean like the heaven's parting or a big rainbow?"

"Something like that," I said.

"When you see nature Justin, do you see the clouds moving sometimes slowly, sometimes swiftly across the sky? Or a single blade of grass growing? Or perhaps the fading sunset? These all are part of a divine plan and order, moving at their own speed, in their own fashion. Our prayers are like that. We give them up to our Creator and then we need to wait for an answer. Sometimes it comes in a few moments, sometimes within weeks and sometimes once in a lifetime. Larry spoke enthusiastically.

"Yes I understand, but what does this have to do with the penny?"

Larry then pulled out the penny he had just picked up outside the restaurant. "Do you see what it says?"

"Yes, of course I do, *In God We Trust*"

"Exactly. Not in government, not in the money upon which it is printed. Not in love, family, or nations, but in God. The one thing we will always have. It cannot be taken away, nor can we be separate from it, and especially, most especially when we listen."

"OK, I think I am beginning to understand." I mused and he continued, "What you didn't know Justin was that I had been trying to make a decision about selling my old Karmann Ghia, you know the one that I have had since the 60's?"

"Yes I do, you love that car and I can see how it would be hard to part with."

"Well I have been going back and forth on the decision to sell it, and to let it go. I don't use a stick shift and clutch as well as I did at your age. Just before I arrived at the restaurant I was thinking about selling the Ghia again and I decided it was time. And then within a few moments, we look down and find this penny. To me this is a prayer answered in the affirmative - yes, it is a good idea to sell the car."

Larry gave me the penny with this admonition, "When you are having trouble with a decision, turn it over and see how your prayers are answered. I think you will be very much surprised"

And with that, I silently sent a prayer to God saying, "OK God, I will listen and I appreciate any guideposts, or penny's along my path that you care to send me. Thank You."

It wasn't very long after making my affirmation that I began to find wherever I went, not only pennies, but also nickels, dimes, quarters, and even Euros too! As a seeker on the spiritual Path, always desiring to know God's will for my life, it struck me as a wonderful, yet so simple reminder of my alignment with a higher power. It is said, "It is done unto you as you believe," and so it is with me now as I believe that the found penny is an affirmation that I am on my perfect path. I have been amazed by the ways in which such a simple signpost has helped.

I have shared my penny stories with friends who, similarly inspired, have taken up this idea and now have their own stories of affirmation to tell. My wife Joan took on this concept with enthusiasm as you will see from the stories she shares. We hope when you read our stories they inspire you to play with these ideas and find you are not alone. There is guidance and connection available at your feet if you decide to see it. In this on-going conversation with God, thankfully pennies are plentiful and God is patient.....

Spirit is Talking to Me

By Joan Doyle

A book of stories about found pennies, I think, as I get out of bed. I have my doubts. My husband raves about his found pennies, as he feels they are an affirmation that he is on the right Path! They each say, "In God we Trust," and he is very trusting in God. I've rarely met anyone who believes God takes such a personal interest in what happens to him. I totally love his idea that God leaves us signs and I find my own pennies, but people can be so skeptical when we tell our stories. Even if they believe in God or Spirit, they don't believe God came out of his or her heaven and placed that penny there as a message for insignificant little me or Justin. They smile, indulging their kooky friends, and I can't help imagining they are thinking "These two have bats in the belfry; someone simply dropped it and didn't pick it up!"

So yeah, I have written several of our stories out, but I'm not convinced a book of them would be riveting reading. I love to read inspirational material myself. I think it's a must, actually, if we are to keep guard of our thoughts, and stay in a place of possibility and openness to God or Good or the Universe—whatever you have decided to call it. And yes, we do more than occasionally find a person who has a penny story of their own or a story of how they felt they got a sign of some kind. People on the Path do ask for guidance and even pray for a sign so they can know they are moving in alignment with Spirit and doing what is in the greater good. I remember a woman who found white feathers and believed they were a sign an angel was watching over her and things would work out OK. And there was the lady who found playing cards and felt they had significance for her. The truth is if God is everywhere present, omnipotent and omniscient, then it's totally plausible that we could see his/her handiwork everywhere.

Yes I believe all people are an expression of Spirit, of God, so people can be angels in our lives, and people drop pennies. Spirit works through people. I have certainly been affected by things people say in passing—something that takes me out of my rut of repetitious thinking or petty concerns. Like the older man at the supermarket yesterday. He was just so sweet as he carried the kitty litter to the car for me. He said to come find him in the store if I ever needed anything carried. He was so obliging it made me think what a spirit of willing service—of love to be more accurate—he brought to his job. I was touched by his attitude and it made me want to have a better attitude myself.

Of course I feel I have many angels in my life; I am grateful for that. Justin is a major blessing and a wonderful encouragement to me in all of my endeavors, as even now he extorts me to put our stories into book form.

I'm still not convinced, as I ready myself for my day at the library where I work part-time. Funny, I think, how I resist getting in the shower when I am warm and dry in my bed in the morning, and how when all warm and wet, I resist going out into the cool air to dry off again. We humans don't like change much, do we?! Still, if we stay put, it's not much fun either in the long run. We need variety. Maybe if the book of stories could be more than just about pennies, but signs in general—messages from the universe, love notes from the ever-present Spirit in a myriad of shapes and manifestations, maybe then I could get behind it. I've certainly experienced those in many forms. Maybe today I can be more watchful. What we look for we find; I am familiar with that idea. I often tell the people I counsel to watch for love in their relationships—to be love finders, instead of fault finders. OK, I'm decided; I am looking for Spirit's guidance, looking for a sign that this is the way to go with my writing.

I reach in the closet for my denims. I like this idea of watching for the good in my life. I think it's bound to increase my happiness whether I write the book or not. I stick my hand in to flatten the pockets of my denims. What's this? There's a laundered and folded paper in here. I pull it out. It's a ten dollar bill. God! That's better than a penny; the higher the denomination, the more resounding the YES! I can't wait to tell Justin—talk about an instant answer! Thank you Spirit.

And just in case I was in any doubt that I got full approval for a book about the universe's messages to us, this was not the only sign I got that day. When I got to work at the library, the very first book in the pile to be checked in on my arrival, out of all the possible topics, was, "Finding a Literary Agent." And with that book was a bookmark inscribed with a quote from St. Francis de Sales. It told me, "Make yourself familiar with the angels, and behold them frequently in spirit; for without being seen, they are present with you."

I am listening and I am heeding the direction I am being given as I write down these stories. It is my hope that you may be inspired also to trust that there is help and guidance available to you, too, if you choose to believe and be watchful.

Tennyson wrote,

"Speak to Him thou for He hears, and Spirit with Spirit can meet. Closer is He than breathing, and nearer than hands and feet."

I would love to hear your stories. You may e-mail me through the book's website, www.SpiritIsTalking toYou.com

Sign

By Amanda Sargenti

"Change is the only constant in life," is a famous saying I try to live by, and that helps me put things into perspective when I feel I need to color my life differently. When it's time to make changes I often tend to favor the ripping off the band-aid technique. Since I tend to lose my equilibrium and inner harmony when assimilating changes in my life, why not change everything all at once? Sure, this temporary sense of insanity is by no means flattering to anybody, but at least I can give myself a break, knowing that I am trying to run a marathon on quicksand.

When living in Monterey, California, a few years back, I was flirting with the idea of changing my life one hundred percent. By this I mean: changing jobs – preferably careers, moving back down south, and ending a long relationship. Changing my immediate environment constituted not only leaving the majestic ocean and lusciously green, famous cypress trees but also an eclectic and genuine support system of individual souls.

I decided to drive to Los Angeles to visit my brother in the hope of buying some time before needing to make these long overdue life-altering decisions. After getting into my car and driving on a windy road towards the freeway, I began setting my intentions for this trip on which I was embarking. All of a sudden I remembered something I used to ritualistically do whenever I felt the blanket of confusion wrap around me. When the going gets tough, I ask God and the Universe for a sign—some sort of confirmation or guidance. Even though I usually enjoy a challenging and analytic, even cryptic thought process, I suspected my feelings of uncertainty to have clouded my vision and ability to filter in any insight. Paralleling the mind of a banana slug or maybe even an amoeba (with all due respect), I summoned my heart energy together and pleaded to God and the Universe to please send me a sign to work with, something that would help clarify the path I was meant to take. I remember advising the Universe to be gentle with me because I was in no state to dissect any abstract hints from the beyond. Understanding the importance of being specific when asking for a request, especially when involving the Universe and God's help, I recall humbly asking that a "foolproof sign" would be granted to me. By this description, I hoped that I would be given a "sign" that did not need much interpretation or analyzing.

Just as soon as I set my intentions and verbalized my heart's desire, a big truck coming out of what seemed left field, blended into my lane, forcing me to halt. Before I could even react to the dance my car was involved in with this truck, I started to laugh, close to hysterically. Much to my amazement and disbelief, there was *one* word written in large red, bold letters on the back of this truck that demanded my attention. Any ideas what this one word was? Of course...the word was no other than "SIGN."

Sometimes I can't help but laugh at the absurdity of life... "SIGN?" "Really??" "What sign, and for what?" I soon began to ponder. Well, once again, the Universe gave me exactly what I had asked for...nothing more, and nothing less. I had asked for a "simple and obvious sign," one that did not need any interpretation.

Even though I did not have any clarification as to the decisions I needed to make, I did realize two things: how quickly God and the Universe respond to us when we are in need and reach out for help—if we listen and are receptive. The other reminder was for me to keep and strengthen my faith, to remind myself that although I don't have (and probably never will have) all the pieces to the puzzle of my life, I ought to be confident and never forget that no matter what happens and despite what my perspective on life might be, I am guided and loved by God and the Universe. I was then; I am now, and I will always be. You, too, are loved by the same Universe and can feel guided and connected if you just listen and allow yourself to be molded by the natural flow of things.

I Am Here and All is Well

By Sandi Duncan

It was New Year's Eve 1990, going into 1991, and I was on my way to a peace concert at St. John the Divine in New York City. It was freezing that night; the temperature was sub-zero and there was a biting wind. I was tempted not to go out, but Kathleen Battle and Odetta were singing. It was one of those concerts you just didn't want to miss, so I was braving the elements to be there.

My partner and I grabbed a cab and were hurtling across a darkened and pot-hole ridden street when we hit a large bump in front of an old abandoned church. Being abruptly jarred into the present moment, I looked up and there, perched on the eaves of a decrepit church, was a beautiful white dove. It is unusual to see birds at night but particularly so on a freezing December evening in New York City. And its appearance was all the more startling, because it was the very symbol of peace and I was on my way to a peace concert. As I looked at this magnificent bird, I had the thought, "Maybe this year is about finding inner peace, and this dove is a reminder for me to focus on that in the coming year."

All through the concert I kept seeing the image of that white dove on the darkened eaves and it continued to haunt me for weeks to come. Its message of finding inner peace also gnawed at me until finally, in February, I made a decision.

I was talking with a friend about being uncomfortable in my life. I'd just come back from a vacation in Florida and was already planning my April and October vacations. I lived for getting away from my life in New York, though I had a great job and salary, many friends and social activities, and I was singing in one of the top concert choirs in the city. But something was missing, and I couldn't identify what that was.

My friend asked me to quickly tell her, without thinking about it, what I'd like to change or do in my life if work, my relationship and money weren't a factor. My immediate response was, "I'd move to California," to which she replied, "Then you must go."

Two months later on April 8, 1991, I left New York City at 5:00 pm in my new Toyota Corolla wagon with my partner, two cats and all our plants. We arrived in Los Angeles on April 18th, found an apartment in Los Feliz and moved in within a week. We only knew three people in Los Angeles and neither of us was employed but … we were living in California!

In June, I was still unemployed and my money was running dangerously low. One day, while sitting parked in traffic on the 10 freeway, I began talking to God as I tend to do when I'm in my car. I asked, "God, was this move a big mistake because I don't have a job and the money is almost gone?"

Out of nowhere a white dove appeared, circled my car three times and disappeared. It got my attention! I remembered that this year was about finding inner peace, and I was already where I wanted to be, so it was simply a matter of time before things turned around.

Within an hour, I was home and the phone rang. A woman who'd been a client of mine in New York was calling to find out if I was still looking for a job. She then directed me to call a friend of hers, a producer of an NBC show, who might be able to help me. Two hours later I was in his office and he was offering me a job.

White doves have mysteriously appeared nearly every time I've had a life crisis where great faith was called for. I saw one the day I found out I had cancer, and over the six-month treatment process they seemed to be everywhere. They've even shown up when I've needed to make smaller life decisions. When I couldn't decide whether to take an apartment, a dove landed on the wire right over the apartment while I was talking to the landlord. A dove even appeared over my head at a Dodger's Game when I was field producing a segment for a TV show. I couldn't find the camera crew two minutes before the event started, and was getting worried that I wasn't going to be able to get the footage I needed to complete the segment. Within seconds of seeing the dove, I heard a man ask if anyone had seen the NBC field producer; the crew I'd been expecting had been replaced by two freelancers I'd never worked with before, so I had been looking for the wrong camera crew. Once we got to work I was able to land and shoot more interviews than the person who normally covered celebrity events.

Over the years I've had a few naysayers tell me that white doves are everywhere, that they are used for release at weddings and at Dodger games and often don't find their way home. That doesn't matter; they can be everywhere for everyone to see, and still they hold a special meaning for me. Whenever a white dove appears to me it's a visual reminder that God is ever present. It's as if God is speaking to me and saying, I am here and all is well.

A Blessed Meeting

By Joan Doyle

A penny on a lunch table on a Saturday in June, I didn't know then how significant that was. I was lunching with a man, a casual acquaintance, nothing romantic, though I was single and looking for Mr. Right. We had met on Match.com a year before, had decided the other was not the one and opted to stay in touch since we had similar interests.

"Oh look, a penny," he remarked with a delight that I found unwarranted. "We are on our perfect path!" He went on to explain what a penny meant to him and I liked the idea. We had just visited a spiritual center he frequented which I had been curious about, and I thought the penny sounded like a lovely sign of affirmation. Like a signpost saying "YES, KEEP GOING THIS WAY." Our lunch came to an end, and as we began to shift focus to our separate day's plans and prepared to part like we had done on our three or four meetings over the previous year, I said, "I'm going to an art fair, just for an hour. I'm thinking of taking part in it next year; do you think you'd like to come along?" He hesitated a moment and then said, "Yes!"

Well, the Fair led to a visit to a park and then to dinner under a full moon, and later to flowers and other dinners, to a ring and a romance like I'd never imagined. It led to a relationship like no other I have experienced, so how could I possibly have imagined it? Out of the blue I found what I was looking for right under my nose! What prompted me that day to invite him to the fair? What prompted us both to say yes to all that followed? Being open, right timing, having done the work of our separate pasts, letting go of judgments or preconceived notions, listening to the angels whispering in our ears?

Daily we make decisions, sometimes the decision not to decide. So many factors affect that decision, and subsequently, the outcome of that decision. If we are to make instant decisions that enhance our lives, I believe we have to cultivate the more conscious decisions and actions we take in the spirit of love—love of ourselves and of others. In the same way that meditating daily can affect the quality of our thoughts during the day, being conscious in our decisions, making choices based on love and not fear, means we lay down the thought patterns that serve our automatic responses. Our habits, consciously developed or otherwise, inform those split-second choices. It's why we do the work of self-development—to enhance our lives.

I asked Justin to join me at an art fair and he said yes. Both our life experiences came into play; but there was a third component, in my opinion, for we would both agree that our small selves are not so wise. Our Spirit selves guided in that moment and brought us the best gift we have ever experienced: each other. Making room for Spirit as we let go of control only enhances life. And pennies to affirm our direction—how perfect!

The Divine Speaks to Me in Songs

By Kristina Kiefer

When I got it into my head that I was going to India to participate in a spiritual course, I did not know exactly why, or what I was searching for. That was the year I was supposed to go to Australia, not India. The previous six months I had been planning to travel to Australia at Christmas with my brother and parents to visit my younger brother and his family that had moved to Australia last year. So I did not expect to wake up one morning just knowing that I was going to India, as if I had always known that and it had always been a part of my being.

So there I was at the Oneness University in India wearing all white clothing, most of it bought in a quick shopping trip to Macy's in October, grabbing whatever I could find in white, even if it was one or two sizes too big. I thought I had a relationship with the Divine. I was in for a big surprise, because I was to see this in a whole new way as a result of this trip. It happened during one of our first visits to the Oneness Temple; we were doing a process that is intended to strengthen the relationship with one's Divine, whatever the Divine is for each person.

We were at the end of the process and I lay down on the cool marble floor, with my head on the travel neck pillow that had become my constant companion. In the serenity and peace, a song popped into my head and just stayed there; it was that song by Meatloaf, "*Two Out of Three Ain't Bad.*" What the heck! I was supposed to be having a sacred experience—where did that song come from? I could not get it out of my head and it was driving me crazy. The lyrics in my case though had a slight twist. I attracted men who loved and needed me, but did not want the relationship that I did. I woke up several times that night, and the first thing I heard in my head was the lyrics again, "*Two Out of Three Ain't Bad.*"

Again, it was there to greet me in the morning, and by the morning break I was singing other words in my head just so that I would not hear those lyrics. In the afternoon session we did a process to heal relationships with spouses. Not being married, my focus was on relationships with past boyfriends, and I reflected on the hurt in those relationships. I wished to heal the pattern of disappointment and repeated failure. It was then that the song hit me over the head. I understood what the Divine was trying to tell me—that was my theme song! I had been in too many relationships in which I did not get the love I needed. It was if a dam had burst, and I cried and cried. I went through the healing process with the other participants, and the joyous dancing and release at the end. While I was dancing, I told the Divine that I needed a new song; he had to give me a new song.

Later that night we went to the temple, and there was a period of time when we were just waiting in a foyer. As I was sitting there, I felt the energy of love all around me and the Beatles' song, "All You Need is Love," popped into my head and stayed there. The presence of love grew stronger as the lyrics repeated. All I need is love.

All I need is to be the love; yes, that's the experience for me! From that point on, "All You Need is Love" became my theme song—so simple. It was also the beginning of a more personal relationship with the Divine, in which we sometimes laugh together and speak to each other with songs. There is a song by the group "Live"—"*Dance with You*" that is my latest favorite to share with the Divine.

Until the experience in India, I did not get it when people said that having a strong personal relationship with the Divine was the quickest route to awakening. It is still a journey for me, but at least now I realize that in oneness with the Divine, there is oneness with all beings, and that is what I live to experience each day.

Unique Expressions

By Joan Doyle

My eyes were filling with tears as I made my way down the sidewalk of the main street of my village toward the supermarket. When I reached it, I could not go inside in the emotional state I was in, so I veered off toward the outskirts of the town. There I knew I would have no witnesses but the cows, who taking a cursory glance would return disinterestedly to munching the lush Irish grass. The emotion of leave-taking was surfacing and would not be contained! My parents had lived in this village for over 50 years and my childhood had been spent among its people and its beautiful countryside. I had gone away to boarding school when I was twelve, and since then had only spent two more years living there. But those short years growing out of that earth, years of belonging and identity, had kept drawing me back and had grounded me like nowhere else on this globe over the decades to follow. And now, after 15 years of living in Los Angeles—which might as well be an alternate universe to this location—I had brought the love of my life to my home place.

We married in the presence of my family and those of his who had been able to travel. It had been a most happy and emotional time. Justin had returned a week before me and now it was my turn to leave. As usual I was desolate.

I often compare this transplantation of my body to my second home in America to an organ transplant. On returning to LA, there is the possibility of rejection of the new country within the first week! And no matter how often I go through the process, there is always that transition time. But now, for the first time, I was returning to my husband. And this did change things.

My heart held the happiness of my return to him and the sadness of my leave-taking simultaneously.

As I walked, teary-eyed, my sadness dominant, I thought of asking for Justin's patience and understanding on my return. I would ask that he not be offended if I was blue for a day or two, that I was happy to be back but that I needed to let go gradually of my home and family. It was when having this thought that I found a penny! I stooped to pick it up off the old stone paving and smiled, feeling reassured. Justin would sometimes quote his Dad, "When in doubt, communicate." Justin was teaching me much about communication, and this penny was saying, "*Yes, talk about it.*" Holding things back can lead to misunderstandings. I knew as I looked at this shiny Irish penny that there would be times in our marriage when our separate life experiences could lead to misunderstandings, but that if we could communicate, everything could be worked out.

Two people, no matter how close, or in tune, or in love, are completely separate individuals and won't always understand each other. But if there is a willingness to share, especially when we feel vulnerable, and a willingness to listen lovingly to our partner without judgment, I feel that the relationship can grow and flourish. Allowing the other to simply be a witness to our personal processes, we allow the other to give us the gift of love in the form of their healing presence. I believe this ability to be there for each other is more powerful than we can imagine. This is the safe place that Justin and I have agreed to create, and it draws us forever to each other.

God Shows Up in the Most Amazing Places

By Dean Regan

God is everywhere present, shining forth as all things seen and unseen. And still, in this cacophony of brilliance, there are moments of shimmering clarity when our awareness—our consciousness, if you will, that God is everywhere present, is made even more conscious.

God has given me the gift to be able to entertain people— sometimes through singing, sometimes through acting, sometimes though dancing, sometimes through a combination of all three. Recently, on a drive from Los Angeles to Palm Springs to rehearse a musical project with some wonderful fellow-artists, I became aware of what a beautiful day it was. The car I was driving in was comfortable, the weather was crystal clear, there was a feeling of openness to the day, and a readiness to welcome creative exploration at the base of the mountain range nestling up to Palm Springs.

Ahead of me on the way to rehearsal was a car; the driver was not visible, the car unmemorable. But on the bumper was a sticker that called out like an orchestra reaching a dramatic crescendo: "Love People. Cook for Them a Wonderful Meal." In that moment, I related to that bumper sticker idea. Not so much because of the cooking aspect–I don't really cook–but because of the way we show our love to others. I realized that I show my love for others by singing to them; the more the merrier—the more songs, the more theatres, the more churches, the more people. In that flash of an instant an idea came to me for the "bumper sticker expression" that has been and continues to be the purpose of my life—"Love People. Sing them a Song."

There are two types of people in the world: those who appreciate refrigerator magnets and those who don't. I am a proud member of the former. My refrigerator is covered with magnets for cities and activities.

These days my primary channel for entertaining people is through solo concerts. I sing at performing arts centers and the larger cabaret rooms across America, as well as church-related events. And occasionally I perform, quite literally, around the world. At my concerts I have a booth of items for sale to audience members, both so that they can take the concert "experience" home with them, and also so I can celebrate and contribute to my artistic affluence. That day—my sunny, free, Palm Springs rehearsal day—I had been thinking about a series of refrigerators magnets that I could share with the folks who enjoy my music. And that is when God showed up as the bumper sticker on the car in front of me which helped me to crystallize my whole life purpose as an artist: to show my love for people, I sing them a song. And, thus, God showed up on that bright and sunny day in so many ways, but one was an idea that is easy for me to hold in my heart and share with others.

So, if you come to one of my concerts or listen to my music online, I hope you feel that sense of love that fills my heart every time I sing. And remember to do your own version of "Love People. Sing Them A Song." What's does your refrigerator magnet say?

An Avalanche of Nothing

By Joan Doyle

Once upon a time I loved having e-mail. I badgered my sister in Ireland to get a computer so we could be in touch on a daily basis, in the days prior to Skype or texting. "Please" I begged, "We can e-mail every morning and night instead of only talk once a week by expensive phone call. We will feel closer, like we used to be."

Today, I hate e-mails. No one reads them fully anymore. If the subject line doesn't give the message in short-hand the e-mail is likely to drop down in the list un-read and quickly it is forgotten. Right? I suppose I am guilty of this too on my busiest days and for many of us that's everyday. As a freelance artist, counselor, writer and library page, weekends can be work days too. Unlike in a time, long past for many, when a single nine to five job designated time to work and time to play. Now everything gets blurred into one continuous networking, texting, e-mailing interaction with friends, family, clients and potential clients, websites and blogs, chat rooms and virtual shopping carts.

Internet addiction is now becoming accepted as a very real problem. Avoiding the real world, impairing short term memory and decision making abilities, (so I read on the internet!) addicts feel a need to be in communication even when there is no message to convey. Relationships instead of deepening become more shallow as people accumulate an impossible number of friends on Facebook. Bite size pieces of information from many sources suffice while lengthy meaningful communication with a few is forsaken.

Personally I am burned out. I have expressed a wish to my husband recently to go on a silent retreat. I have had a strong desire to disconnect and to re-connect to something real. I have been missing my family in Ireland a lot. The love I feel is very real and unchanging but the sharing of meals, milestones, lengthy phone calls and most of all time, has diminished. I have been struggling with the acceptance of that and its inevitability after eighteen years abroad. I am the one who moved so far away, so I take responsibility and acknowledge that everyone, including me is overwhelmed these days.

This morning as I walked my dog Otis I could feel my irritation about this situation fuelled with thoughts like, *I am always the one to pick up the phone and to travel the six thousand miles to see my family. No one had come to see me in the last five years and as for phone calls there is nothing but dead air. I'd hear no news of home if I didn't pick up the phone myself. Would anyone even notice if I stopped calling or visiting?* Feeling very sorry for myself, I wondered was I wrong to wish someone would call *me* for a change. *Was it too much to ask?*

As I had this thought, I recalled at least two friends who had shared with me that they felt the same way; that they were always the one to call either friends or family. Maybe everybody feels this way. Maybe all of us are making calls to people from whom we wish to hear, and at the same time getting calls from people who we don't regard as essential to us, so we discount those calls. That idea made me smile as I thought of all the disgruntled people not seeing the good they have but wanting what they don't; a very human condition.

Just then a California bluebird flew out of the tree I was passing and landed to the right of my path. My smile broadened to a laugh! It always delights me to see a bluebird, for one thing, it is rare and for another they always remind me—*"the bluebird of happiness is in your own backyard."* I needed the reminder this morning and I am glad for how Spirit uses nature's messengers. I was reminded I am responsible for my own happiness and I choose once again to simply count my blessings; an age old wisdom that never looses its effectiveness.

In truth I get great pleasure out of calling those I love and I choose to stay focused on that. When I feel lonely I can remedy that by reaching out to someone else. When I take the focus off of "poor me" I quickly realize there is so much need in the world and I have something to give. The love and connection I wish to feel is in the giving and I feel it when I care for another human being, or an animal or plant, or my home or myself. I don't have to be rigidly focused on my family; I am surrounded by people whose day I can brighten as I brighten my own by connecting with them. It is up to me to bring balance to my life and remember what is truly important and meaningful. The internet is a tool and I am in control of how I use it.

As Marcus Aurelius, stoic philosopher, so wisely put it *"Very little is needed to make a happy life, it is all within yourself, in your way of thinking."* The world of a thousand things, as delightful as it is, can be a distraction, an illusion, an avalanche of nothing, depending on *your* way of thinking.

The Queen

By Joan Doyle

It was June 2009. Recession, foreclosures and unemployment were the predominant news items in the U.S. and Europe; in fact, people across the globe were affected in some way by recent economic events. Work-wise it had not, so far, been a good year for me in Los Angeles. With ample time and not a lot of money, I managed to travel to Ireland to celebrate my parents 60th wedding Anniversary. It was simply an event that couldn't be missed. It was a joyous occasion, which my parents anticipated with delight and enjoyed thoroughly, despite my mother being wheelchair-bound and having other minor health issues. Seven of my siblings were present, as well as their various spouses, and sixteen grandchildren. There was singing and eating and speeches galore.

I had a little over a week to savor visits with my family amid the lush overgrowth of the Irish summer. Every wild plant was at its peak, lavish and exuberant with blossoms and foliage. I was lucky to be experiencing a week of sunny and dry weather, hoped for all winter long by the Irish, but often barely glimpsed between the nimbostratus and the stratocumulus layers of cloud that lie like cotton wool blankets on the emerald land.

Of course this was how I recalled my childhood summers: wandering in shorts from the village to the sandy river for a cooling swim; or playing tennis on the street during Wimbledon season, and coming home with shoulders sunburned and hungry for salad sandwiches make by my mother from the fresh and wholesome produce of our own garden. A visit home was always crammed with reminiscences, and on this morning as I walked home from the village with the newspaper, I longed for those simpler and carefree times.

I was finding it hard to keep optimistic about my work situation as I thought about returning to LA. Just then my eyes fell on a large coin in the soil at my feet. It was not an American penny and did not have those words, "In God We Trust," but it might as well have had, for I relate all found coins now with that message and the origin—the universal divine. I picked it up. It was an English fifty-pence piece, more than an inch in diameter with seven sides and depicting Queen Elizabeth's profile. Quite unusual in these parts, as Ireland has used the Euro since 1995 and has always had its own separate currency from Britain.

I looked at the Queen on its face and it reminded me of a book on CD I had listened to years before called "The Stages of Man." It described the stages of a man's life, and how he is a prince during his thirties as he builds his kingdom, but in his late forties and fifties, he is established and is the king of his realm. At this stage he needs a queen to share it with. A woman getting involved with a man at this age needed to understand how a Queen acts, and that she now needed not so much to nurture and support the career-oriented prince, but to increase her ability to receive the bounty shared joyously by the King. I connected this story with the Queen on the coin, and my message was clear.

I needed to trust that I was receiving from the universe all that I needed, and more. I thought of my loving family, the festive celebration, the joy and abundance of Ireland's bountiful summer, my delightful husband back in my other home in California, and I began to feel wealthy. A verse came to mind, *"Consider the lilies of the field, how they grow; they neither toil nor spin; yet I tell you, even Solomon in all his glory was not arrayed like one of these."* Security is not found in objects or things. True security is found in knowing who we are, as children of the universe, heirs to all of its goodness, if we will but receive.

I needed to feel worthy to receive, like a queen must feel—deserving and loved. I looked at the Queen on my coin and I said a silent, heartfelt, *"Thank you."* Remembering the bad news constantly in the Irish papers and on radio, I thought, *"Spirit is my source. I see its bounty everywhere and my need for food and shelter are met today. That's all I need to know. Thank you, I receive with gratitude the bounty shared joyously by the King."*

This was the truth then, it is the truth now and is always the truth.

Listening
and Allowing

There is guidance for each of us
and by lowly listening we shall hear the right word.
- Emerson

Listening is a broad category of communicating with the Divine because we cannot heed any guidance unless we are willing to listen. Listening has within it an intention to hear. It is most often done in solitude. Walking in nature, meditating, reflecting over coffee in the morning, doing mundane tasks, all are ways in which we might be receptive to guidance.

In a situation where we are upset or feeling strong emotions, it is good to look at what it is we are thinking and how we speak to ourselves in our minds. Ask if this thought is loving or supportive of ourselves or others. When we take the time to stop and listen, it allows a spiritual element the space to make a marked difference in the daily and ordinary events of our lives. Be willing to simply be willing. Soften your attachment to particular outcomes. Be present to what is.

Instruments of Love

By Laurie St. Clare

I feel awful; I just want to stop crying but the tears are relentless. I'm finally being swallowed up by my sadness and fears. I am alone and flailing to stay afloat. I cannot stop hearing the words and feeling the frustration of my friend, Rachel. We'd had words and even though I could see her point, I felt terrible for me. I'd been staying with her since I moved out of my home I'd shared with my husband for the last seventeen years. It had been five months now and although she had said I could stay much longer, I didn't know how I would be able to.

As I lay awash in my own grief at my displacement in life, I knew that Rachel was under extreme pressure at work. It would have been easy to rail against her and take my anxiety out on her. I was the one whose life was in complete upheaval! I asked for help in seeing the best of the situation, to be guided for both of our highest good. I started to relax my breathing and focus on love instead of fear. I tried to stand outside myself and see myself, as well as Rachel, as the Angels see us. We are beings that need love but we are also, very importantly, instruments of love. I knew squarely in my heart that she was having a difficult time, and my being here was an added stress to a place of sanctuary for her.

Rachel worked extremely hard in a stressful environment that provided relief for people in crisis. I realized her blow up had more to do with things she was going through at work. She was an amazing woman and friend going through her own tough time. I drifted off to sleep feeling compassion for her and myself as well.

In the morning I stayed in my room to give her space as she

34

got ready and left for work. I thought about how I would be able to spend my day in this quiet home and tend to my needs, while she had to go back into a highly stressful situation. I felt a strong sense of love well up. I wanted her to have peace. I wanted her to know she was special. I realized we all have difficulties, and me feeling sorry for myself and only seeing my needs made the world a cold, small place. I knew this was not the truth and I wanted her to know this, too. I made the decision to send her flowers at the office. I had an arrangement of gorgeous flowers delivered to her.

Rachel called me later that afternoon gushing with gratitude. She told me how lovely the flowers were and how everyone at the office had been uplifted. Our differences melted easily away. Love filled in every crack pain had opened up. I felt empowered by my ability to be open to love, to give it and receive it. I had been guided to choose love, to feel it, to express it and act upon it. In choosing love I also affected all those people at her work place.

Seeing my friend as me, as another being that is just like me, experiencing hurts and fear but also encompassing the beauty of the Divine gave me the ability to act with compassion. I had asked for help, gone into myself, connected with love, and acknowledged unity instead of separation. That is "Spirit." That is "Love." That is you and that is me.

A Poem from a
Deceased Loved One

by Sean M. Kelly

Over the years I've delivered a lot of professional development training courses to companies in Ireland and abroad. On one particular occasion I was getting the room ready to deliver a stress management course for a large Irish bank. Phil, a lady from the bank who was helping me to set up, told me that the husband of one of her friends, Joan, had just been diagnosed with cancer and had been given three months to live. As my father had died from cancer, I felt a lot of compassion for Joan and her husband facing this huge challenge. Three months passed, and I heard that Joan's husband had died almost three months to the day after the diagnosis. This, of course, stirred up more feelings of compassion within me. I had also recently finished writing a book about my dad dying from cancer and what had happened in my life subsequently. I felt a nudge from the universe to send a copy to Joan even though I had never met her!

When faced with decisions like this, our rational mind will often try and put us off the idea—the *"what will the neighbors think?"* sort of mantra! *"I had never met Joan, so who was I to send her a book I had written? What would she think when she received it from someone she didn't know?"* Well, sometimes we have to *"walk on air against our better judgment,"* as the Nobel Prize-winning poet, Seamus Heaney, so wisely said. So I decided to walk on air—I posted the book to Joan. I also had to give the book with no conditions attached. Sometimes we give things to people expecting something in return, and if we don't get something, we resent them. This is a very limited and unhealthy form of giving. When thoughts of, *"I wonder what Joan thought of the book,"* or *"I still haven't heard anything from Joan,"* came to mind, I had to remind myself to be totally detached. I had to leave it in the hands of the universal intelligence, God. I was simply playing my part. Of course, once we detach from the very thing we sought, it often comes to us anyway!

After a number of months I received a lovely letter of thanks from Joan, and I felt I should return the compliment. Synchronistically, at the time I was learning about angels and how they can help us in any area of our life if we ask them for help, and also how they often send us guidance. The trick is to be still enough and aware enough to hear or feel this guidance.

The following Sunday morning I awoke at about 5 a.m. and just lay in bed allowing thoughts and inspirations to come to mind. As I thought about what I was learning about angels, I wondered if it would be possible to write poems for people who had lost a loved one as if that poem came from their deceased loved one. *"Well, I have written poems in the past for the family of a friend who died, and for my own family on the first Christmas after our father died,"* I thought, *"so yes, this is possible."* My rational mind then came back in with, *"Oh Sean, go back to sleep; it's too early!"* Still I could not get back to sleep. *"Go on downstairs and have a go,"* my heart was prompting me. After a few more prompts, I got myself out of my warm bed to have a go.

I thought I would write a poem for Joan from her deceased husband. It was a lovely, bright summer morning. The house was really quiet and peaceful. I lit a candle and sat at our kitchen table. I asked for guidance and let go of any personal agenda. The only intention was to capture in words what I felt most guided to write. The poem flowed absolutely effortlessly, and when I had written it, I was delighted because I felt I had really captured the two messages—Dave was still with her, and it's ok to have another relationship. Now what about the title? The first one that came to mind was, *"To Joan from Dave,"* but then my rational mind kicked in—*"Remember, you have never met this person; what will she think when she receives a poem from you as if it's written by her deceased husband?*

It's totally crazy, Sean!" I quieted that side of my mind and asked the question, *"If I were Dave, what would I like the poem to be called?"* Immediately I knew; I would call it, *To Joan from Dave*. I wrote a short cover letter for Joan and sealed the poem in an envelope, ready for posting. The letter was hanging around the house for a few days before I posted it. Again I had to remind myself of unconditional giving. I was simply being a messenger. However, I still wondered what she thought of it; did it help her? *"Oh, my God,"* I thought, *"I hope it didn't upset her!"*

A couple of weeks later, I received a message on my mobile phone from Phil, my friend at the bank who had originally told me about Joan. I wondered why she had phoned me, as I knew she was on holiday. At the time I was in a playground with my children and suddenly just wanted to go home! My rational mind started going crazy with thoughts like, *"She's heard from Joan and is wondering if I am some sort of 'nutter',"* or *"The poem has really upset Joan and now everyone in the bank knows, and I'll never get work there again!"* I started giving out to myself, thinking things like—*"I'm getting out of all this psychological, psychic and angelic stuff; it's totally mad and a complete load of rubbish! That's it. I've had enough!"* After about twenty minutes of mental turmoil and sweat I managed to get Phil on the phone. This was the conversation:

"Hi, Sean."

"Hi, how are you, Phil?" I awaited her reply.

"Sean, Joan received your poem."

"Oh, did she? Great, and are you enjoying your holiday, Phil?"

"Sean, did you know anything about Joan before you sent the poem?" Phil asked.

"No. What do you mean?"

"Well, the very day Joan received your poem she was going into hospital for surgery for breast cancer, with which she'd just been diagnosed! Your poem really helped her and gave her great strength, as she felt Dave was with her."

Her words sent shivers down my spine; but I will also admit

they were a bit of a relief, as they meant I hadn't upset Joan. Well, I really didn't know what to say. I was absolutely and totally amazed. How could all this have happened so perfectly? Who orchestrated such perfect synchronicity? Would it have happened if I hadn't followed my heart and sent the book about my dad? Would it have happened if Phil hadn't asked me to deliver a course for the bank? Would it have happened if I hadn't got up out of bed that morning to write the poem? Would it have happened if Joan hadn't met Dave?

The truth is I really don't know. However, it was a great example of the infinite loving and organizing intelligence of the universe.

Not long after that, Joan wrote to me about the whole experience, and thankfully had fully recovered from the breast cancer.

It's such a wonderfully strange and mysterious world! What must we do? We must allow ourselves to be used as instruments of the universal intelligence. Is it always easy? Not in my experience. Is it incredibly humbling and fulfilling? Absolutely. Will you touch people in ways that touch on the divine and the miraculous? Absolutely you will. What do you need to do? Follow the promptings of your beautiful heart.

The Wukoki Bee

By Julie Penman Livesey

It was more than seventeen years ago. I was traveling around Northern Arizona with a friend, and this particular day had found us wandering around the Wupatki National Monument—a large area of desert northeast of Flagstaff—where remnants of ancient pueblo settlements belonging to the Anasazi and Sinagua Indians had been preserved.

Early October, the temperature was in the comfortable upper seventies, allowing two sun-deprived Brits a rare chance to develop a pretty decent tan while moseying around the various ruins.

The impressive three-story Wupatki Pueblo, having once been large enough to house as many as three hundred people, sat majestically on the edge of a small plateau overlooking unobstructed views of the Painted Desert to the east. We spent an enjoyable hour there before jumping back into our hired car and heading off to what we soon found to be the most striking of all the sites open to the public—the Wukoki Pueblo. Built onto an isolated block of sandstone, it loomed out of the distance like a miniature Ayers Rock. There was absolutely no other structure of any significance as far as the eye could see, natural or man-made—just miles and miles of arid scrub-covered desert.

As we stepped out of the car and began to approach the ruin, the deep red of the Pueblo's brickwork and the surrounding sand and rock that had produced it struck a huge contrast with the dusty green of the dry and prickly scrub growing out of the sun-baked ground. The only sound to be heard was the gentle rustling of a light breeze through the brush and the crunch of our hiking boots on the dusty path. We were truly in the middle of nowhere.

We left each other to our own thoughts as we rambled around the site, taking photographs at every turn. Though we were the only people there we felt no sense of unease at the isolation of the place and soon split up. There was an abundance of specially created paths around the pueblo for the tourist to follow, but I soon found myself wandering off the designated path in order to get the perfect picture.

I weaved through the scrub, stopping intermittently to look through the camera lens, before moving on to the next spot, and the next. I could sometimes hear the distant scrunch of my friend's footfalls as she meandered amongst the ruins, but I felt in no particular hurry to rejoin her.

I don't know what made me turn around. One moment I was crouching down and aiming my lens at the tower which appeared to grow seamlessly out of the rock before me. The next, I was standing with my back to it and staring down at the ground a few feet ahead of me. A little bee (of the fluffiest bumble variety) was running across my path as fast as his tiny legs could carry him. I barely had time to register the fact that he wasn't flying when I spotted a small lizard in close pursuit. Instinctively, I took a step forward, and to my utter amazement, the bee immediately made a swift and perfect 90 degree turn in my direction. The lizard, sensing my presence, hesitated, continued the chase, then hesitated again, not sure of what to do.

I decided not to take any chances. I picked up a long thin twig, one of a multitude scattered around me, and touched one end of it to the ground. The bee ran straight for it. I watched in awe as the little bee wrapped his front legs around the twig—then hung on for dear life, as I hoisted him high into the air before gently plopping him down onto a nearby flowering bush. The lizard, thwarted, made a hasty retreat under a rock.

Bending over to inspect my new friend, I could see no obvious sign of injury, but did notice that he seemed to be carrying half his bodyweight in pollen. Was this the reason he hadn't simply flown away from his pursuer? Had he been just too darn heavy? I guess I will never know.

I left him there on the bush to rest, hopeful that he would make it back to his hive safely, and as I walked away, I couldn't help but marvel at what had just happened. This tiny creature had literally put his trust, and his life, in my hands. What strategic genius, what courage under the worst of pressure it had taken to hope that his best chance of escape from the clutches of a giant monster was to hurtle himself toward an infinitely larger one.

I am not religious, but I do believe in a Universal Energy that connects us all. Most days, so much goes on under our very feet that we are totally oblivious to, but on this particular day, out in the Arizona desert, I was made fully aware of our wonderful inter-relationship with even the tiniest of our co-inhabitants here on Earth.

It was more than seventeen years ago and our connection was only fleeting, but I still remember that little bee of the Wukoki Pueblo.

Trees

By Joan Doyle

It was Christmas Day. I was far from family once again and finding it difficult, as an emigrant often does on holidays of this kind. This year was somewhat different; this year I was with Justin. It was our first Christmas in our new home and we were feeling very grateful for our many blessings. We took a walk after dinner at Wildwood Canyon which is a favorite hiking trail of mine. I would hike this trail three or four times a week, at one time.

There was an evergreen tree there, a Coast Live Oak, and I always lingered to enjoy its beauty and its shade. I felt we had become good friends. How beautiful and regal it looked as its intricate age-old branches spread and hung down in a canopy of leaves. I was often filled with awe by the energy it seemed to exude, by the perfection of nature. A broken branch or two did not take from its majesty. Spending time in the crook, where its main trunk split into three sturdy branches, I felt grounded.

The tree was easily over a hundred years old. Wild fires had burned around it, leaving it untouched. The hillside behind it had slid in the rains and raised the earth around its base making that crook more easily accessible to me. I occasionally had to share this space over the years with ants, and sometimes, with a hive of bees that nested there. I didn't mind. I knew this tree was here for everyone, giving of all that it possessed, unconditionally. To me it represented Spirit as nature, and I sometimes wondered if trees looked on us humans with equal awe! After all, we can walk around and we are equally magnificent in our individuality and intricacies.

I had decided it was the tree's stoic silence that made it the perfect friend. I remember whispering secrets to it as I lay against its comforting bulk. After a break-up I had told it of my heartache, and when I met Justin I had told it of my joy.

On this Christmas Day I had taken Justin there to introduce them, and as I leaned against it to say my goodbyes I thought, "What a friend a tree can be!" At that, I glanced down and my gaze fell on a penny on the woodsy brown earth. I picked it up with the joy of knowing its affirming message, "YES, you get it; you get what I am trying to give to my most precious sons and daughters." We can find love if we look for it, even in a tree. In my loneliness I found comfort there. In my joy I found a friend and a feeling of oneness with life. To me this tree is a reflection of my own flawed yet perfect nature, and allows me to see other people that way, too. Life lessons from a speechless tree; it's all Good, all God if we choose to see it that way.

Sally's Pink Roses

By Sandra Phillips

Learning to listen to my guide continues to be a colorful and interesting journey for me. The messages can come in from completely left field leaving me gawking in wonder at what spirit can do—both bringing a tear to my eye and sometimes leaving me in fits of giggles. Passing my favorite flower stall just around the corner from my Dublin-based studio, I was daydreaming about how friendly my neighbor's cat had been that morning. Now that she had begun to befriend me, there was a lovely connection between us. Earlier this year I had put on my vision board that I'd like to become friends with "a loving cat." My apartment is rented so we are allowed a dog but not a cat. I missed the cat energy around me, so why not simply create a space where one falls in love with me. And this had happened clearly with "Little Paws," the tiny female cat who would run over to greet me and hang out.

The flowers I was passing caught my eye; they were so fresh and colorful. Clear as day the signal came in to *buy my first client, Anita, a bunch of flowers*. I had been thinking of Anita for about three days and felt that there was something really difficult going on in her life—a heartbreak of some sort. Looking at the flowers, I felt an urgency to buy pink roses and pink peony roses and wrap them up together. I knew, for me, that this was a symbol from the world of spirit, connected to a loved one, wishing to pass on a message. Who was it in Anita's case, I wondered? I felt it was a female but I didn't get any other images, just a feeling of pure love and peaceful serenity. I knew that when I connected to Anita, her energy was full of pain and upset, but there was no clear indication for me who this female energy was, that was telling me to buy flowers.

Back in the studio I arrived seconds before Anita. She came in looking dreadful, eyes red and puffy; she burst into tears.

"Oh Sandra, I'm just in bits today. Sally died last night." I looked at her.

"Oh my god Anita, I'm sorry to hear that," I reached up and held her in my arms. She wept. I still didn't get any idea of who Sally was. I kept thinking of "LittlePaws," which all made sense when Anita caught her breath and shared that "Sally" was her cat.

She told me the story of how Sally had a fit and died right beside her. She had felt her go and it was really difficult. She *was* in bits about it all. After a little while, and when Anita had caught her breath, I gave her the bunch of pink roses.

"I got these for you, Anita, they are from your cat, Sally." She stopped and looked at me, and I went on to explain that pink roses are the sign I get when someone passes away.

Anita still looked amazed. I went on to explain that I had been paintings the night before and the image was based on power animals that have connected to me. For some reason, a black puma kept trying to leap out at me to paint, but it wasn't part of the story I was hoping to tell. I believed now that this was Sally trying to reach through from spirit to her—Sally was a black cat. And my neighbor's cat too had been on my mind. So in spirit Sally and I were connecting through all sorts of images in my environment, while I had this feeling of pain across my heart and a knowing that Anita was heartbroken.

I told Anita, "It's possible that this was Sally's way of saying, *I love you, I am okay; I made it over."* I believed this, but I wasn't sure Anita believed that this was spirit at work.

Some days later I got an email from Anita, both thanking me for my support and letting me know she felt much better, that the grief was moving on. She'd had a moment when everything connected together for her. She had been washing dishes at the kitchen sink overlooking the back of her garden. She was thinking about the roses I gave her and what I had said. She saw that the spot where Sally was buried was overlooked by a rosebush spreading and abloom right then with, guess what, pink roses!! She wept as it all sank in; Sally was ok! Upon reading the email I smiled. There really are no limits—even cats can organize stuff in the world of Spirit.

A Talent Multiplied

By Joan Doyle

The rituals of Catholicism were mesmerizing to me as an impressionable child. My favorite was what we called Devotions. Frankincense and myrrh billowed heaven-ward in clouds as the incense burner swung in arcs from the hands of an acolyte. From a balcony, the unseen choir elevated the atmosphere, their ethereal voices chanting the haunting, monophonic, melody of the Latin hymn, "Tantum Ergo." In red ceremonial robes the priest, his shoulders, arms and hands wrapped in a humeral veil, held aloft a gold crucifix with a sun at its center, called a monstrance. With this he blessed the congregation. My senses exalted by these sounds and scents, the experience imprinted itself deeply and profoundly in my memory.

The focus of reverence at Devotions was a large, thin circular wafer otherwise known as the host, or the Blessed Sacrament. The host, blessed by the priest, represents the body of Christ. It was exposed in the glass center of the golden monstrance.

My first religious experience involved the host. I was seven years old. The receiving of the body of Christ is known as the sacrament of Holy Communion, and a child first gets to participate in this ritual when they reach the age of reason. At seven it is deemed you know what you are doing. I had been well prepared and evaluated for my readiness.

I was dressed in the white silk dress worn by my two older sisters before me, and a short veil, white gloves, sparkling white ankle socks and sandals, to reflect my purity. I felt very special. As I had been taught, I visualized taking the hand of the Virgin Mary as she led me to the altar to receive the host for the first time. I took it into my mouth, and without letting it touch my teeth I swallowed it as I returned to my seat. I knelt and prayed, and when I sat up in my seat, I felt as if I was filled with light and floating above my seat. I felt happy, holy and most serene. I don't remember when the feeling subsided but I never told anyone about the experience.

I kept silent about a great deal as an introverted young girl but I gave much thought to the ideas of my religious education. There was one parable from the gospels that gave me particular concern. It was the parable of the talents. In it a man is preparing to leave on a journey. He chooses three servants and to the first he entrusts five talents, to the second, two, and to the third, one talent. The first two servants quickly set to work to multiply their master's money. The third servant does not invest the money; he digs a hole in the ground and buries it. When the master returns, the first two servants are commended as "good and faithful servants" as they increased their master's wealth; both were invited to share in their master's household. The third servant is chastised and sent away because he had only preserved the master's money, not multiplied it.

It seemed a little unfair to me: he did take care of the money and returned it. Discussion was not really part of the teaching process back then, so I made what sense I could of it. I took the meaning of the story to be about the using of our God-given talents, and at that time I was becoming aware that I had a talent for art. My teacher, Mrs. Barrett, had said so. She had allowed me to restore the faded illustration of the seven days of creation that wrapped around the classroom. Naturally, I was delighted and loved every minute of it. My classmates continued their lesson. As I walked to school I contemplated with some concern how I was going to use this talent in the world. I did not know one single professional artist. What was I going to do with my talent? Would it end up buried and would I then be sent away from God's house and banished from His presence? It was a weighty issue for my eleven-year-old brain.

As it turned out it would be another ten years before I took an art class, and though I forgot about the parable of the talents, I never forgot about my love of art. Like a penniless child drooling at a candy store window, I looked longingly into the art classroom every time I passed it. I studied the academic subjects my parents had chosen for me. When it came time to choose college, all I talked about to the career counselor was art. I applied to an Art program, but my portfolio was so sparse I did not get accepted. I studied Agricultural Science, biology being one of my best subjects. After I failed Microbiology on my second attempt, I recognized that I could no longer leave my art talent buried. I worked up a new portfolio and this time got accepted onto a design course. Making up for lost time I graduated top of my class and never looked back.

Art was pulling me as the moon pulls the tides. This is how it is with the things we truly love in our lives, with our purpose, with the thing we are born to do and with the thing that makes us feel most alive. My ideas about God have gone through vast transformations since my childhood, but some of the messages are still the same. Spirit is constantly nudging us toward full expression of our talents, and when we are involved in them, we are truly in the flow, authentic to who we are, and also most of service to mankind. This is true communion with the Holy Spirit. What is more inspiring than to see someone enthusiastic and passionate about their pursuits, whatever they might be? What is more satisfying than feeling fully expressed and on purpose?

Spirit/Consciousness/God flows into what we do through our enthusiasm and enjoyment. If we deny ourselves, we hold back what Spirit wishes to be expressed in this world through us. No one else can bring into being what is uniquely ours to do. I have often felt like I was not good enough as an artist, but at some point I had to acknowledge that though I may not be as skilled as some I admire, I am more accomplished than others. What I am is, perfectly me and that is always good enough.

We can't be banished from God's presence by not multiplying our talent, as I believed as a child, but we can banish ourselves from a feeling of being fully alive by being overly self-critical, by comparing ourselves negatively, and by asking "who am I to do this thing?" Who we are to do this thing is the Living Spirit within us. Our job is to get our "bloated nothingness" out of Spirit's way! Is there something at the back of your mind that has been pulling you for a long time? Maybe it's time to stop holding back and get in the Spirit of living more fully! As my mother loves to say—there is no time like the present.

"Let us take our bloated nothingness out of the path of the divine circuits."
- Ralph Waldo Emerson

Grace

By Sabrina Johnson

The elephants were calling me. I heard them in my dreams. Not just any elephants, but the elephants in Thailand. It started when a young woman I knew went to Thailand on a volunteer vacation to work at an elephant sanctuary. I wanted to do this. The call of the elephants was like a shofar sounding to announce my personal Jubilee Year. This Jewish tradition from many pasts ago would be announced with the trumpeting of a ram's horn as the commencement of forgiveness. I'd recently celebrated my 50th birthday. It was time to take in this grant of freedom and forgive myself for how I'd harmed my body with excess weight so that I could barely move for much of my life. It was time to rejoice in the freedom of being able to move with ease, and to celebrate the work I'd done on many levels to shed the excess burden.

Twelve weeks before I left for Thailand, I created a sacred covenant for my trip. It was my agreement with God as to how I was to engage on this journey. The purpose of my covenant was "Grace," inspired by God's promise from John 1:14: *"And the Word became flesh and dwelt among us full of grace and truth."* The way in which I agreed to live God's promise was set forth in my intentions: "I revel in the physical manifestation of the Grace of God unfolding in and as and through me in the form of perfect physical health and wholeness. I consciously and joyfully dwell in this living temple of God, my body... I AM a loving, compassionate witness as I acknowledge the material world and engage in the absolute Divine."

With this covenant, I traveled to Thailand as a mentor to teenage volunteers under the auspice of the Power of One organization. Their mission is to teach teens that they can make a difference. They taught me this as well. After arriving in Chaing Mai in time to celebrate the New Year, we took a bus up into the jungle hills to spend eight days at The Elephant Nature Park. The Park is a sanctuary for elephants that have been abused, neglected or abandoned. I knew answering this call to help heal the elephants was also self healing, for I too had been physically abused as a child.

One day I watched an extraordinary woman train the elephants to obey commands such as to lift a foot for inspection or allow an examination of their ears and trunks. Elephants are so large that they cannot be safely anesthetized, and so in order to treat them, they have to train them to allow access to their bodies. Using a clicker, a stick, and pounds upon pounds of bananas, this woman teaches the elephants to obey her spoken commands. When the elephant obeys, it's given a banana. The trainer told us that the elephant we were watching, Mai Thai, had just started. They'd tried training Mai Thai a year earlier but couldn't because "she was going through an emotional breakdown, in grief. Her best friend died and she went crazy." This is how deeply, madly these elephants love each other.

The following day, I studied one elephant as she put her weight on the left leg while attempting to hoist her right leg one step ahead. She dragged it, and then leaned onto the lamer right leg and shuffled the left leg ahead. I knew this walk. I started walking like this when I was ten years old due to a childhood bone disease. I had Teflon pins put in both hips to keep them in their sockets, but I still limped. After 40 years of abusing my body with excessive weight, my right hip collapsed and I had it replaced. I now walk with a slight hiccup of a hitch in my stride.

Seeing this elephant, whose name is Medo, struggle as she walked, I imagined how others felt as they watched me shuffle and drag my elephant-sized body mass. Sometimes strangers would stop and ask me if I was in pain. I was, but I ignored it. Now, witnessing this elephant, my body remembered that unacknowledged anguish as Medo and I became kindred spirits. For a brief moment, it felt as though her body cellular energy meshed with mine. It was as if I could feel the throbbing burn and sting that accompanied her movement searing through my body. It was the residue of suffering that I had ignored and numbed with food. These few minutes of discomfort, however, were followed by a new awareness of how far I've travelled from the limping shuffle and drag of my body—and my spirit—with which I'd walked through life. Realizing this, I forgave myself and others for the harm inflicted upon me, just as I forgave those who harmed Medo, knowing we both had been given the freedom to live in sanctuary.

A few days later, we headed south for our last week in Ban Krut, where we'd spend our time at local schools teaching English. At the last school we visited we were given big name tags to wear, as were the students. I looked around at the smiling faces and their names. Here's a short list: "Unplugged," "Mild," "Sense," "Boss," "Mind," "Gift." I asked these students if they understood what their names meant in English and they did. They understood that they had the freedom to choose the name they wished to answer to. Later that day someone told me that in Thailand, they do not have a common agreement of what a person's name should be. Rather, they choose a name by looking at a word and deciding if they like it.

A few months after my trip, I remembered that day with Unplugged, Sense and Gift. I thought of how our group, strangers to each other before this trip, were bonded together now like a herd of elephants as we traveled our paths. And, I thanked the elephants for showing me how to love uncon-ditionally. Having been subjected to hurt and neglect, they did not become hurtful or neglectful. Rather, they love one another deeply with hearts that can break if their loved ones suffer or die.

I then realized that I'd been granted my Jubilee promise, God's promise of Grace. Grace, to me, is living from that place of true forgiveness and love, with gratitude. This is what I know as true freedom. So, in the Thai tradition, my new name is "Grace." And I answer as Grace, whether it's Spirit talking to me through elephants or any other sentient being. For now I know the Word of God is the Spirit of God that dwells within me, within the flesh of my body temple. This is who I really am, a spiritual being through which Spirit expresses Itself ever so gracefully as the loving being that I am, grateful for this journey that continues to eternally evolve.

A Day Off

By Joan Doyle

It was a day in October; I could see a grey misty cloud clinging to the hills as the sunshine created a beautiful contrast of light and dark that can only be seen at this time of the year in California. I was between jobs, the intermittent state of the freelance artist. Always during the down times I have a list of personal goals to attend to: a new website to design, personal art work waiting for just such an opportunity to be created, update my show reel, flyers to create to promote a new class I am about to offer—not to mention jobs around the house; the list is endless. I become driven, with an "I must be productive" mantra. I had been slowly working through some of these tasks for about a week, creating more work as I went it seemed, but achieving some part of what I'd set out to do.

This morning a feeling that often surfaces during these periods was gaining hold. Lethargy, a mild depression, a desire to just do NOTHING! I could not find the motivation to do anything; it was as if my muscles were saying NO! And the rest of me was saying, "But you can't just do nothing; there are goals you have set yourself; how are they going to get done?" Then the judging voice—"You are lazy, out of work; do whatever you need to do to get motivated!" All of these harsh voices created in me a pressure that was counterproductive, and more importantly, created a discomfort and unease that I knew could not be good for me. A friend called, and feeling very indulgent, I agreed to meet her for a midmorning walk and talk in the park.

Playing truant spilled into the afternoon as we talked up a storm, sharing stories of our challenges and our plans, our frustrations and our triumphs. Prolonging our time we went for tea at a nearby café. All spent and very happy, at the exit of the cafe I found a penny. I explained to my friend what this meant to me—"We are truly on our perfect path," I said. "I am being reminded to trust in God, in "good," and also that God is not only the external God, but also internal—God in me, as me. I have honored that part of God today by choosing to take this time off. After all, we are the ones creating our own experiences so why not create pleasant ones when we can. It seems so simple and obvious but sometimes we forget to give ourselves permission to just *be*. It was the best thing for my wellbeing, on this particular day."

The next day, with renewed energy and motivation, I took on the world again as if I was a new person. Rather than making myself conform to my ego demands, it was more healthy to listen to the quiet demands of my soul. My mind is so limited in comparison with Spirit's understanding of what it is that I am needing. My penny was my affirmation that I took the right action. Resisting stopped the flow of creative energy and created anxiety. Going with the flow—letting it be—allowed the energy to move again. I hope next time I can recognize with less resistance or guilt that I can take a day off and play.

Guidance in Decision

By Justin Elledge

I was concerned when I became aware of Ted's occasional habit of drinking before he came to work. In this environment, he was a hazard to himself and a possible danger to students. We worked in a design college woodshop teaching students to use the saws, sanders etc., as well as methods and costs of producing their designs. Ted was a new hire and I was still getting to know him. He was retired from his former life of being an automotive repair technician and he was very knowledgeable about circuits and electrical systems. The company he had worked for had changed over the years as electronic systems became more and more replacement-oriented rather than repair-oriented. For this reason he was retired, and replacing the faulty components was turned over to younger and less technically-challenged individuals.

In describing his former life, Ted occasionally waxed melancholy, lamenting about what a great job it had been and that he had felt challenged and useful in his career. Retiring in his mid-fifties, he felt he still had much life left in him. From what I observed he seemed competent and good with the students, however, I was concerned his drinking might cause him to injure himself, or even worse, allow a student to become injured.

I am not sure if it was his life circumstances that had led him into heavy drinking, and perhaps drinking had led him to be retired, but I feel it may have been the former. At least that way I felt I could have the least judgment about it. It was difficult for me to confront Ted considering my own father's alcohol abuse and how that had affected me, however, there were present issues at hand to deal with, and safety on the job was paramount. I wrestled for several days on whether to confront him directly about his drinking, to inform a superior, or simply keep my mouth shut and my eyes open to any hint of danger to him or others.

Finally, one evening his drinking was so obvious I had to do something. I prayed for guidance on what to do. Should I report him to our supervisor, guaranteeing his dismissal, or speak to him directly, not knowing how he would react. I was crossing the room and observed an air hose lying on the floor. I looked down to avoid tripping. Stepping over it I came to the conclusion to address this issue directly. I continued for a few more steps and I made a cut on the panel saw, finished, and turned around again approaching the air hose on the floor.

As I walked over to the hose, watching it to avoid tripping—there, right next to it, where I had walked only moments before—was an extraordinarily shiny penny! I was amazed, as I was the only one who had just crossed this way and there was no way that anyone could have dropped it in such a short time. This coin simply had manifested in answer to a prayer, as an affirmation of my decision. I picked up the coin to feel its hardness and the reality of it. I held it close, and then and there, walked over to Ted to discuss his drinking. No yelling, no reaction of rage or denial. I said my piece and he promised it would never happen again. And to this day he has never gone back on his word. Thank you Spirit for your guidance; three lives were blessed that day.

Open Channel

By Joan Doyle

A good friend repeatedly told me about a church her friend attended and raved about. I had been looking for community in the sprawling urban jungle of LA, but from what she had told me this church seemed too "out there." After all, cults and sects abounded in these heathen lands – at least that's how this innocent foreigner saw it. It's amazing I left Ireland at all but I was feeling stuck and throwing myself in the deep end of the unfamiliar was my way of breaking free.

Resisting it all the way, I did go to the church with my friend and surprised myself when I kept going back. It was literally love at first visit. I found what I had begun to think did not exist: a community founded on universal truths common to all major world religions, which made no other religion wrong and no person undeserving of love.

Cautious at first I began to take classes in their philosophy and gradually I allowed myself to bask in the delicious acceptance and encouragement I experienced. I had always been shy, introverted and lacking in confidence but for the first time in my life I could feel myself begin to blossom. In the safe atmosphere my teachers created, I gradually began to accept that I had value and I could feel myself embodying greater confidence. My study of Spirit, as expressed through each of us uniquely, had a very definite practical element which I loved. If I was a channel for good/God/Spirit then I needed to allow it to flow by following my heart and letting it inspire me to action. "Faith without works is dead," was the idea that spurred me on to do what I never imagined I could do.

I decided to do a marathon. I had imagined this was beyond

me, but now with my new knowledge of how Spirit works it came within the realm of possibility, simply because it called to me. I chose to listen.

I selected the Dublin City marathon for the cause of arthritis, as my mother and aunt both were affected by it. As well as the arduous training involved I would have to raise $4000. I had no idea how I was going to do that but I though if others have done it, then it is possible for me. I had set my intention; my work now was to eliminate the doubt that could stop my progress. I had to counteract thoughts of "this is too much for me" or "who am I to do this," with encouraging words. When I was running alone and I was feeling tired I would repeat, "I am the lightness of God, I am the strength of Spirit." I was amazed how effective this was. When I hit the long slow hill on my route I proclaimed "the hill and I are one!" It worked.

When it came to sending out letters asking for financial support I found I had all kinds of judgments about what I thought people would give. I also felt bad about writing begging letters. I knew that was no attitude in which to achieve my goal so I began kissing each envelope, sending it with love regardless of what came back. Interestingly the people I imagined would give generously gave $10 and those I thought might only be able to give $10 gave $100. It illustrated to me how limited my own thinking had been.

One petite mentor I had during training, Lillian, was eighty one and had the spindliest legs you can imagine. She'd point at her legs, standing before us now in heels, and say, "You think these legs got me over the 26.2 miles? No!"

She'd wag her finger at us, pausing for emphasis. Then she'd point to her head, "This is what got me there."

Lillian was a true example of *whether you think you can or you can't, you are usually right.* Not believing in ourselves can deprive us and the world of all manner of good. After months of preparation, it was a proud day for me when I crossed that finish line in Dublin.

Any endeavor coming from the heart is made easier knowing you are supported. My confidence in the transcendent Spirit, and myself as its channel opened the way for this achievement and for so much more.

Is there something in your heart that you would like to allow manifest through you?

Direct
Communications

Anyone, at any place and time, can have direct and immediate access to the central truths and experience of life itself.
- Emerson

When we pray, we are beginning a dialogue with God to which we hope to hear an answer. There are prayers that are spoken wishes. There are prayers that are pleading and begging for something from an all-powerful entity outside ourselves. There are prayers as simple as "Thank you." There are affirmative prayers that assert, positively, the truth of who we are and what we are heir to. My preference is for the last form but whichever we choose we are opening to communication with the Divine. We wait for guidance or an outward manifestation of what we desire to experience. The more we take time to communicate with Spirit, the better the conversation. It's like any relationship: rapport is built on mutual trust. Asking is an action that represents trust in a response. So don't be shy. *"Ask and it will be given to you; seek and you will find; knock and the door will be opened to you."* Matthew 7:7.

Speak to your highest self—ask what would love do, ask what it is you need to know, ask what is the highest good for all—and know we may not always get what we want but we do get what it is we need. Trusting that Spirit is expressing through all circumstances and people perfectly you will know you have gotten your answer when you sense a shift toward feeling safe, loved and peaceful.

Clearing My Head

By Joan Doyle

Striding down the road away from the house, I was angry. Justin was late; he'd said he wanted to go walking right after work, before it got dark. The light was fading and while waiting twenty five minutes, not even a call had come in explanation. I could not call him as he keeps his phone turned off while at work. I'd prepared a salad for us, for after the walk, and I had worked hard all day too. It seemed I was the only one caring about our evening's plans.

We were not long moved in together at this stage and we were still working out our routines. I knew he was probably just delayed by a last-minute task at work but I felt let down, ignored and forgotten—however irrational that might be. I knew I was over-reacting as Justin is reliable, communicative and very considerate, yet I was enraged and couldn't seem to help it. If he showed up then I would probably be silent and sullen and our evening would be ruined.

All I could do was walk, and walk, hoping I would calm to a rational state. Even understanding why I could be annoyed, I couldn't understand why I was feeling so deeply hurt. On top of that I was making him into a villain—thoughtless, uncaring and self-absorbed. I needed a talk with myself.

My arms swinging, I reminded myself of Justin's good points, his past loving gestures and kind deeds. It was having little effect. It seems I wanted to be mad; it felt justified somehow. I could not let go of it and I wanted to hurt him back. Let him find the house empty when he gets home and wonder where I am! I must have walked a mile at this point and I stopped to sit on a wall, catching my breath. Sitting there I silently begged to have these uncomfortable emotions taken away from me. My cell phone rang. It was Justin. He was on his way home; he'd been delayed at work and wished he was walking with me. Without speaking of my feelings, I suggested he walk toward me from the house and we would meet.

As soon as I got off the phone I remembered something I'd read. When we have an extreme reaction to some minor slight, ninety-five percent of the emotion is from some ancient hurt. I felt the truth of this statement then, and knew I'd felt let down, ignored and forgotten as a child. Growing up the seventh child of nine, that was not too surprising, but it had had its impact. So what do I do with this knowledge? As I walked very slowly in the direction of home, delaying my meeting with Justin, processing emotion and thought, I could feel the anger gradually replaced by sadness. With the gentleness of the adult I now was, I began to speak softly to that hurt-child Joan, still within me, acknowledging her and saying I was sorry she'd been hurt. With each footstep I felt lighter, and soon I knew I could talk to Justin now, calmly and without accusation. His actions may have triggered my feelings but he was not responsible for them. I began to look forward to seeing him, and when I saw his distant silhouette in the dimming light my heart filled with love.

I knew he wanted to walk with me, I knew he meant me no harm. As we came together and he turned to walk in the same direction as me, I took his hand. At that same moment I saw something shining on the sidewalk. With delight I found it was a quarter with the message, "In God We Trust," and knew this solitary walk was what I had needed.

Having taken responsibility for my emotions, finding their true source and worked with myself in gentle loving kindness, I was now free to see the truth of the current situation. As I examined the shiny coin in my hand I noticed the word Liberty, and thought, "the truth will set you free." The found coin confirmed this for me; I was on the right path to freedom and love in the self-reflection I had done. If we are caught up in old emotion we relive the past, no matter what the present looks like. In releasing it we are free to be in the present and fully present, which opens so many more possibilities of new and more wonderful life experiences. I like being free.

The Path of the Butterfly

By Justin Elledge

Some years ago when I was thirty-two, I found myself unemployed, without a home, and not knowing where my next paycheck might be coming from. Then, through a stroke of good luck, some friends of mine were planning a trip to North Carolina and needed someone to watch their house while they were away. They would be gone for a month to take care of some legal issues regarding real estate, and they asked if I would be willing to house-sit for them during that time. As my schedule was so open, I agreed and had an entire house with a wonderful garden all to myself. Heaven! In addition, the prior owner of the home was a Reiki Master and healer who had created a beautiful home and garden. While staying there for those few weeks, I experienced a wonderful sense of life and renewal.

Earlier that year, I was more than a bit melancholy, feeling I had come to an impasse in my journey. I lacked any direction in life and felt abandoned by God. A few years prior I had unintentionally lost a great deal of weight, and try as I might to gain it back, I remained rail-thin. My family was concerned, not knowing what to do and I felt depressed. Doctors had many medical tests performed, which ironically showed me to be in perfect health, with no explanation for the weight loss. Everybody thought it was great that I could eat anything and everything I wanted and still stay slim.

During the second week of my stay at my friend's home, I found myself sitting in the back yard, enjoying a perfect fall day. The sun was shining, birds chirping, and it seemed as if I had not a care in the world. I found myself praying and just a bit angry at God for my life and all of the physical pain I had endured. A thought occurred to me. I needed some sign that there was some plan in my life, some reason to continue on, no matter what the struggle, no matter where life would take me.

So looking around the backyard garden, and not seeing any burning bush, I held out my hand and said out loud: "Dear God, if you have some plan for me, I need to know it. I need something real that I can see and feel."

I then looked around the yard and I saw a small yellow butterfly flitting around the flowers, unaware of my presence. I then said in a humble tone, "If you are real, God, and have a plan for my life, please have that butterfly come over to me and land in my hand." And then it happened. The small creature drifted over to me, and ever so gently landed in my left hand. And for a moment I held my breath, and said nothing, not wanting to upset this miracle before my eyes.

I then, doubtfully and out loud, said "I don't believe it." And with that uttered, the butterfly lifted up, unconcerned, and flew away heading back across the yard. At which point I immediately said, "I believe, I believe," and as only moments before, the butterfly then returned to my outstretched hand, as softly and quietly as any angel's wings. I was stunned and sitting there afraid to breathe; I felt warm tears falling down my face. The butterfly sat quietly in my hand, calmly, without fear, as if it had all the time in the world, its small feet barely registering on my skin and weighing nothing—so fragile and unafraid.

It was then that a sense of awe and wonder like nothing I had known came over me. Who was I not to trust my life to something greater, as this butterfly did so willingly? I knew it was my trust that was the issue. With this prayer answered, I knew I could trust God. I knew that Spirit held me safe, that I could rest there until my own wings were strong enough again for me to fly.

The butterfly sat there in my palm allowing me to feel and see a presence, through the sobs and sniffles, without any fear or concern. For a full minute or two, I saw and felt that small creature, and knew that God was real, as real as *it* was. I felt that no matter what direction my journey in life would take, I was at home and had found peace in the certainty of my connection with something much greater than I, and there was a reason for me to be here.

A Prayer in My Pocket

By Joan Doyle

I feel very fortunate to have a prayer partner in life. Long ago I had a friend who was a recovering alcoholic and she had a mentor through Alcoholics Anonymous. I envied that she had this type of support. When life got stressful, day or night she could call this person who was experienced with her type of struggle, and she could rely on his calming words of wisdom. I suppose parents could fill that role but I never wanted to worry mine, especially my Dad, who was a worrier. Friends could fill that role, I suppose, but for me after my training as a counselor, I needed someone who saw situations from the soul perspective so I could find what I needed to learn. Friends were great when I wanted to get into the drama of the situation and have them get angry on my account, labeling the other person bad for upsetting me. Sometimes that feels very gratifying but I don't learn much from, "I'm right; they're wrong." Is this not the attitude that has been the cause of wars and endless strife down the ages? On the path I have chosen there has to be a better way, so when I want to find that way it is my prayer partner I call.

As part of training in Spiritual Counseling we were partnered up with someone to practice our craft of affirmative and healing prayer. When we pray we affirm what is our Truth—that there is only one source of all life, that its energy is for good and that we are inseparable from it; it is who we are. Not unlike the Star Wars' salutation, "May the force be with you!" We say the Force is always with us. No matter what the outer circumstances look like, they have no solidity; they shift and change. We affirm the changeless. It is our rock. We don't magnify the undesirable circumstance by focusing on it. This way we are making room for the good to come into being. We affirm what it is we wish to experience, keeping in mind the good of all people while knowing all is possible in Spirit. We give thanks for it. Then we release the prayer and wait in trusting expectancy.

As one of our teachers in the Science of Mind says—"How do you expect to see heaven if you keep saying it's not here?" For example; a relationship ends and we moan and despair of ever finding love, while in truth, love and hope spring eternal. It looks like we are out of money but the universe is absolute abundance, we just need to see it all around us and start the flow by giving. We can always find something to give; our time, our kind words. We give from the infinite source that we are; knowing there is more where that came from.

Just as the body sometimes needs treating so does the mind, our prayers are called mind treatments. We treat, align our thinking with the highest truth, then we move our feet, meaning, we take actions trusting in a good outcome. It's simple and profound. When the prayer is answered, we call that a demonstration. This is the part I love about my "mix and match" religion, as some people call it—we expect and acknowledge results. It's a very practical philosophy.

My prayer partner and I talk on the phone twice a week. We talk and conclude with prayer, every time. It's as if we wrap up our trials and frustrations in a love blanket of powerful words and recognitions of boundless possibilities and let them go. We see for each other what the other can't see. I always feel better after exposing my human thinking to a loftier consciousness! I really do feel fortunate to have a prayer partner in life.

Last week we both had astounding demonstrations which we could not ignore. Very often it's easy to take it for granted when good things happen. Most people would say, "Well that would have happened even if you hadn't prayed." It comes down to what you choose to believe and if it works for you. Prayer works for me. No matter what is happening, I always have affirmations of my truth, like a prayer in my pocket—*God is the Love that I am,*

Nothing opposes a Divine idea, Spirit is the source of my supply, All is unfolding for the greater good. It feels much better to fill my mind with powerful thoughts than to fret, to worry or to get angry. If that's what you are choosing to do, I have to ask—how is that working for you?

"What?"

By Sabrina Johnson

I know that Spirit is always talking to me—gently guiding me, lovingly nudging me as to which direction to go, comforting me when I need it, inspiring me when I desire it, and touching me always with a soft silence that speaks louder and with more clarity than anything I can describe with words or imitate with sound. All I have to do is be still and listen, knowing this is so.

When I was asked to write about how Spirit talks to me, I thought I could write a whole book—and I am doing just that with a spiritual autobiography. Yet once again Spirit touched me with its silent presence and told me exactly what to write about.

It was one recent weekday morning on my commute to work. I was stuck in traffic on Beverly Glen Boulevard, one of three main canyon arteries between the San Fernando Valley and Beverly Hills. I sat all tense and tight behind the wheel, thinking, "Why me? Why am I being subjected to this?" That feeling of victimhood came and went within seconds as it transformed into "should haves." "I should have taken Coldwater Canyon instead. Why didn't I? Maybe I should have left ten minutes earlier, or ten minutes later to wait out this traffic? Why didn't I listen to that voice of intuition, to God speaking to me? Or was I just too busy this morning to pay attention?"

As I breathed a sigh of exasperation, I thought of what would await me further along on the road. A car accident? That made me realize how useless it was to feel like a victim, or that I had any way of changing the present moment other than being in it. Maybe road construction or repair was causing the backup. I thought of the men in orange vests working the roads and holding up stop signs or waving orange flags to direct the traffic dribble, exposed to not just the weather elements of rain, cold, or heat, but also to hundreds and hundreds of frazzled and frustrated drivers. I began to feel compassion for those men. I work in an office that is twelve flights above famous Sunset Boulevard, with controlled air temperatures and the somewhat controlled personalities of my co-workers.

Then I went back to feeling exasperated, frustrated and tense, wondering, "Why?" Not exactly "Why me," but simply, "Why?" "What is it this morning that is causing me to be stuck here and now?" I thought of those stories I've read about people in Manhattan who were late for work the day of 9/11 and how they believe that saved them from being in one of the buildings. I thought of how maybe I'm being saved, but then I breathed a deep sigh of agitation and realized that the only saving I needed was from my thinking.

At that instant I heard Spirit's silent presence speak: "You're here to be here, to do what you need to do." Like a kid who pretends they've never heard of their weekly chores, I feigned ignorance. "What? Oh my God, what do you mean, what I need to do? I've already meditated, exercised, cleaned my home, showered and cleaned myself up, packed healthy meals for the day… So what is it??? Oh…Oh," I sighed as I turned off the CD of Jamie Lula signing his beautiful lyrics of, "I surrender, I surrender, I surrender, oh Lord."

In the silence I surrendered as I joined the many other drivers around me, mouthing words out loud. Unlike those drivers speaking into cell phones, however, I spoke into the Infinite Connection of the activity of God, to Spirit. The words I mouthed were prayers of forgiveness and acceptance for my office. Starting with my boss and going clockwise around the office, I recited my prayers for each and every one of my co-workers, their first and last names. As I slowly inched along on the road, passing the men in orange vests waving their flags, I smiled.

My prayers became less of a laundry list of litanies and more of a heartfelt devotion. Pulling up into a parking space in my office building, I finished my prayers and beamed. Mission accomplished! A minute later I waited for the elevator and it immediately arrived to take me on an express ride, straight to the 12th floor. With this same ease and effortlessness, I walked to my desk while having another great silent conversation:

"Good morning, dear God. Thank you, this is Good."

"Good morning, my beautiful Child. Yes, it's all Good."

The Healing

By Joan Doyle

I'd said I wanted to have a healing on that first day, as we sat in a circle on the floor and introduced ourselves to the group. I even remember spreading my arms and imitating the wings of a bird. I wanted to feel freer than I did and to soar, to feel unencumbered by the weight of my thoughts and my history. I remember feeling a bit awkward expressing this to a group of strangers, but I felt I had nothing to lose but what bound me. I was ready to lose that.

It was the first day of massage school. I had driven two hours from LA to Santa Barbara and it was my intention to do this every weekend for the next three months so I could get the training my massage therapist had gotten. Her name was Cody and she was amazing. I would sleep at the massage school sometimes, or at Cody's place. She shared a home with a Buddhist monk who had a temple below her bedroom; I slept on some cushions on the floor. We had to be very quiet and respectful of the sacred space we shared. I felt like a novice, in a world so unfamiliar to me. Cody and I would sometimes meditate on the beach surrounded by the calls of the gulls and the rhythm of the ocean waves. I could feel my life being transformed.

Just six months before, I was preparing for my wedding. My life was looking like it was going to be about raising children with a man of Southern sensibilities. Neither of us had strong affiliations to any religious tradition, though we were to be married in my childhood Catholic Church back in Ireland. I had sought a religious community since my arrival in the United States and there were many to choose from, but nothing resonated for me. There was always some requirement in order to be accepted by their God that I balked at. My idea of God was very broad and unconditionally loving, universal and impartial, where no one was excluded from the club.

My husband-to-be believed life was for living; he was not concerned with existential questions or the existence of the soul. We were not alike that way, but this was *not* why, we did not marry. I admired his self-assuredness, his strength of conviction and fearlessness. He was everything I was not it seemed. I did not really like my own sensitivity and vagueness, my timidity and quiet ways. We had a silent agreement that his way of dealing with life was best, and I should work at being more like him. Naturally, this could not last. Eventually I had to own up to who I was— not so much vague but open, not so much sensitive but receptive to how others might feel. I was an introvert and I would never be brash and bold, except when it came to exploring the hidden world of Spirit.

Six months before our wedding day, I realized I was deeply depressed and that I could not go forward with our planned life. I was plunged into an internal crisis. My rational mind screamed for the sensible thing to do: *he is a good man who wants to share your life forever; you want that, don't you?!* My intuition was firmly saying: *he is not for you; you must let him go. There is another path you must take.* I felt as if I were split in two. My idea of who I was as a dependable, caring person contrasted with this person who could cause so much heartache. There was a lot of guilt on my part, even as I knew I was doing the right thing for us both.

I know now that there are no mistakes, because as I finally owned up to myself and my preferences and allowed myself to explore the world that truly called to me, I found my life increasing in joy daily. It was not through marrying a man who was fearless that I would learn to be courageous; it was by following my own path and speaking up for me. The whole painful experience birthed my intuition. I became very aware of what was right for me and what was not.

Massage school was one of those things. Being massaged all

weekend by my fellow students felt grounding and loving—a wonderful gift to myself. I was reveling in all that I was learning and opening to.

Part of the training included a weekend in a yurt by a small lake north of Santa Barbara. It was here that I had the experience that really allowed me to see who I was. It was a trust walk. Half of the class was blindfolded and the other half were assigned silently to one person each. I was blind to my surroundings. I could feel the light breeze from the lake on my bare arms as my guide took me very lightly by the wrist. The scent of the fir trees and the bird sounds filled my senses as I began to walk in the direction I was being gently guided. My free hand reached out in front of me to assure myself I was not walking into an obstacle. We moved slowly at first. I had no idea where we were going but I was guided to feel a pine cone, a tree trunk and another person. Slowly I began to trust the guide and we moved more quickly. Then we broke into a run. I had no vision of where I was running but in the depth of my mind I saw, as if I was releasing a mantle from my shoulders, all my stories fall away: where I was born, how many sisters I had, when I moved to the US, what had happened a few months ago. I was just here and now. I was free spirit, exploring, running, light and unencumbered—pure presence. I felt excited; I wanted to touch things, experience everything, enjoy the world I was in. It was exhilarating and I totally released myself to the guidance. I was safe. I was pure joy.

Before long we returned to the yurt and I was then required to give my guide a massage, still wearing the blindfold. I had no idea if my guide was a man or a woman but I felt a lot of gratitude as I proceeded to contact the skin of this other body. There came a realization that the body houses this free spirit— one spirit expressing uniquely as each one of us—and that this life is truly a gift to be enjoyed. Limiting this experience by stultifying thoughts and judgments of our selves is a crime against the Truth. I began to cry as I worked, and in my mind I loved this person as if it were myself lying on the table. For I know that we all carry the weight of our past experiences and allow them to limit us when, if we truly knew our own divine nature, we could soar and be free.

This was my healing; this was me, the soaring bird. Maybe not transformed all at once, but now I carried a memory of pure joy and Divine guidance which forever I reference when life threatens to burden me. I know who I am and that I am safe. I know this Truth for you also.

Call Waiting

By Amanda Sargenti

Deciding to take a break from the arduous task of unpacking after having just moved to Monterey, California, I decided to take a relaxing, meditative stroll near the ocean. Contemplatively walking towards the famous Cannery Row, I was taking in all of the visuals, sounds and scents from my new ocean-side environment.

"Thank you, God, for guiding me up here. I am so lucky and grateful for the opportunity to live in a place where other people just have the time to *drive* through." My ongoing dialogue with God begins.

"Beep, beep!" A distinct sound began to materialize near the upper left corner of my mind.

"Ah? Sorry God. This almost sounds like an 'incoming call;' it's the sound I would hear when someone else is calling me when I am on the other line. How bizarrely unusual and how disrespectfully inconsiderate! I am talking to YOU! Who needs to 'switch over' anything when talking directly to the big Boss? Anyway, what was I saying before I was so rudely interrupted? Oh yes…thank you for this clean, quiet and safe new place!"

"Beep,beeep!" There it was again—the same sound disrupting my consciousness, only this time a bit louder and more intense.

"Are you kidding?" I thought to myself. "Am I missing something? I am not actually ON the phone with you, God, so why the call waiting experience? See, this is what happens when I am stuck in a room unpacking and sniffing dust all day! I might be officially losing some of my marbles! Wonderful!"

Before I could continue to wallow in my potential tragedy…

"Beeep! Beeeeep!!"

"OK God, this is not happening! This is ridiculous! I will be back in five. Let me 'switch lines' and see what's the big idea? Either I am hallucinating, or something is somehow trying to get my attention for some reason. I will be right back. I apologize!"

"Beeeeep, Beeeeeeep!"

"Gosh! Yes, ok! Got it! What??! And this better not be a figment of my imagination that's all I have to say, because I just put GOD on "hold" to put my attention here, so…Let's hear it! Good thing no one is witnessing this quiet monologue between me, myself and I, otherwise…!"

Instead of another anticipated "beep, beep," I now received a message in the form of words: "Perfect place for the perfect crime!"

"What?" I thought to myself, instinctively wanting to dismiss this absurdity. Luckily my analytical mind responded and urged me to dissect the situation. As I scanned my surroundings, I realized that the usually densely populated walkway was indeed desolate, with the exception of one man walking way ahead of me.

"Hmm…" I inquiringly began to wonder about this unusual string of events. As I was in the process of gauging my distance to the fellow walker, I soon found myself alone on the walkway, bushes to my right, ocean on my left.

"Well, do I need to worry? After all, I escaped dangerous Los Angeles to be in serene Monterey. In addition, it's not like I've decided to roam around at midnight, it's barely noon."

Even though I was arguing with my own thoughts, I decided to keep GOD on hold to better focus on what seemingly needed my attention. Before I could even formulize a conclusion to all of this, I began hearing a sudden faint rustling coming from the compact and lusciously green bushes on my right side. Even though my focus drifted there, I still attempted to rationalize myself out of the experience.

"Surely it must be a little bird doing exactly what little birds do."

To my dismay, the rustling began to get exponentially louder and more intense until......a six-foot-something man, fully clothed in a light suit holding a brown brief case, jumped out of the exact same spot I was trying to convince myself there was a bird. Needless to say, I felt my heart drop into my gut as my throat tightened. Ok, this is not the time to panic or freeze. I did get a 'heads up' via 'call waiting,' so I should be better prepared to deal with this situation.

Following his jump, the dark man grazed his body across my arm as he, in a deep voice with piercing eyes, mumbled "Hello!"

"Hell no!" I answered him with my silent voice. "This is where I make a beeline and run," I thought. "But wait, don't predators enjoy chasing their victims? Maybe I should walk...! Stop it," I commanded myself. I am always amazed at how many thoughts I can have in a split second. "Maybe I do have some kind of thought disorder? Racing thoughts? No. I am sure this is what they call 'survivors instinct.' Let's think about this. No matter what the truth might be, who jumps out of the bushes in the middle of nowhere exactly at the time when nobody but a female daydreamer is alone?" After quickly gauging the distance I would need to run to get to safety, I began my sprint one large step at a time.

"Ok God, so since you obviously sent an angel to interrupt my connection with YOU, would it be too much to ask to help me out of this situation, please?"

After about fifty "steps and pleases" combinations, I reached safety and entered a neighborhood store. Intending to call the police if this man were to follow me, I peeked out the entrance, and while glancing down the path a few minutes later, I realized that he was nowhere to be found. Running home while out of breath, I concluded my walk the same way I started—"Thank you God..." but this time I added, "... for sending me several warnings (it took a few until I listened) and for keeping me safe."

A Cup of Tea

By Joan Doyle

The silence was deafening when my boyfriend moved out. I rattled around in my empty heart, waiting to hear a footfall or a voice calling out, "I'm home." It was as if I was waiting for life to begin. Alone, all was silence and I, invisible. A long way from home, a year in my new country and the strain of cultural strangeness, abandonment and loneliness pressed in on me.

It was Saturday afternoon after a long week in which I had cried in my office every day, not caring who walked in and saw me. I felt I was holding so much in and I did not know what to do with it. Flailing about in a hell of my own making I wrangled with my choices, berating myself with tortuous critical thoughts. No wonder being alone was something I had avoided. I was between a rock and a hard place, and the hard place was my own mind. Fighting it every step of the way, this experience was breaking down my usual means of survival and I felt threatened, vulnerable and angry.

I had picked up a book of grief rituals at the library feeling a loss of a relationship is a death. Following its recommendation of taking my anger out on some pillows, I had broken open a dam of tears, and yet the pain was not subsiding. Where was the cathartic release it promised? Already on my knees I begged God to take this crushing weight away. I began to feel desperate. I needed a friend. And I needed a friend now!

I called Gary. He lived a couple of blocks away and could get here quickest. He was a sympathetic and sweet-natured guy and I was very happy when I found he was home. "Can you come over right away?" I asked. "I just can't be alone right now." Gary heard my need and very soon he was at my door.

He came in and I immediately began to tell him how I was feeling, crying and laying out my impossible predicament before him. He sat quietly listening as I paced and ranted. I kept thinking, "Make me a cup of tea, why don't you?—that's what a friend would do. Just make me a cup of tea!" Very Irish, I know, not something an American would do as a comfort gesture at all, but that's what I wanted, that's what I knew would soothe my tortured soul. But Gary just sat there. Slowly it began to enter my awareness that Gary was becoming catatonic in the face of my distress.

Snapping out of my drama then, I heard myself say in a calm voice, "Gary, can I make you a cup of tea?" With no help coming from an outside source I had to find it within myself. I also realized my tormented state had brought up for him an old reaction to his schizophrenic mother for whom he had cared in his high school years. In that pivotal moment I learned three profound lessons.

Firstly, I have resources within me that I don't even know are there. There is a witness to my thoughts that came forward as my strength in that moment and it is always there. And this knowledge grew over the months that followed and most especially when I began to meditate.

Secondly, we need each other. Even if Gary couldn't be what I wanted in that moment, he was what I needed, and I could not have seen my own resilience without him. I found I could be a friend even when I felt I had the least to give. I began to see situations that did not look ideal in a new way; there is always something to be known or learned from them.

Thirdly, I am my own best friend. When I made that call and asked for help I allowed myself to be cared for as I was, not composed and in control, but a complete mess, at rock bottom. I allowed Spirit, as love, to enter into my experience and show me what I needed to know. The asking was the important part, in fact the essential part, of the flow of giving and receiving. It is often easier to give, we feel strong and in control. If we don't learn to also receive, we deprive others of a chance to give; we block the flow and miss the opportunity to feel acceptance in our human imperfection. There is strength of a different kind in exposing vulnerability and trusting a friend.

As to the cup of tea, it might not have been what Gary wanted just then, but hopefully he got what he needed too.

When Things Go (seemingly) Wrong

We sink to rise.
- Emerson

From the soul perspective, can things go wrong? I think not. There is a phrase—"My barn having burned down, I can now see the moon." (Basho) It implies that every disaster has some good in it. What we view as something tragic, something we would never wish on our worst enemy, something we dread the very thought of, when it is looked back on, can take on a different hue. I have heard cancer survivors say that cancer was the best thing that ever happened to them. This is not to say that the actual experience of a life-threatening illness is a pleasant one. It may have been permeated with deep fear, with months, even years of arduous treatments, accompanied by depression and lack of motivation or hope. However, people have come out of such ordeals with their priorities rearranged, knowing what is truly important in life. Having faced the worst they are stronger, wiser, happier and more resilient.

In the same way, lesser unpleasant events we face as a part of life also carry a gift. If you have not seen the positive aspect of some past loss in your life, I invite you to ask yourself—do you feel you are stronger for having resurrected yourself and your life in the aftermath of the loss. Are you wiser? Have you grown in compassion for others undergoing similar difficulties? Did the event propel you into some kind of action which you would not have taken had the event not happened?

I know it is not easy to reframe some losses and find the good in them, especially from a human perspective. From the soul perspective even death can be seen as a healing; the individual soul, having completed its earth purpose, continues its journey onward. If you are having difficulties, ask for help. Ask that the deeper truth be revealed to you. Then expect an answer. It may come in some unexpected way.

Rob, A Sufi Soul

By Joan Doyle

Rob appeared before me in a purple tie-dyed shirt and balloon pants in a yellow and blue diamond pattern. Thick wool socks and sandals completed the ensemble. His outfit was not that unusual at Retreat where a large number of people wore purple, but it was distinctive for its random patterns and textures. Despite this conglomeration of color, the most distinctive thing about Rob was his sad-dog brown eyes that seemed to slope away from a pensive crinkle at the center of his high forehead. Everything about him seemed to hang from his thin frame, lynch-pinned at his frontal lobe. It was impossible not to notice Rob, but once seen, it was easy to overlook him. Quiet, unassuming and introverted, he did not push his views, voice strong opinions or initiate discussions. When he appeared before me, I looked into his brown eyes and tried to suppress my judgments of him, to look at the spirit within him and acknowledge it was the same as the spirit in me. I was almost relieved to move on to the next person in the dance and keep on moving.

To quote the retreat organizer, Mary Brenda McQueen, describing the dance, "Heart-Centered Sufi Dancing is a beautiful Spiritual Practice, a meditation of Divine Light and Bliss. We move around the circle from partner to partner, allowing our thoughts to fall away as we experience the Divine in each other. As we connect with our eyes, we do simple, graceful movements while focusing on the positive words of these powerful chants and songs...It is not so much about the dance as it is the Divine connections we make with each other."

My thoughts were having a hard time falling away, but at the same time I sensed divine light and bliss tingling somewhere inside, with the prospect of coming forth into my experience. This was why I kept coming back to these Miracle Retreats, twice a year, Easter and Thanksgiving. Nowhere in my life, even at my church where I found the love and philosophy that changed my life, did I feel the depth of connection and unconditional love I came to cherish from these precious weekends. My husband had introduced me to this group he called his chosen family. I embraced and was embraced by the loving essence at the core of these gatherings.

When I heard that Rob was dying, my heart lurched in shock at the thought of losing an atom in the chain of this collective experience—despite the fact that I hardly knew anything about him; I could not recall a conversation, a shared intimacy, his occupation even. I had looked in his eyes; I had shared the holy presence with him, and one thing I did know was that he loved Sufi dancing. Rob died on March 2nd 2012 at the age of fifty-five. My husband offered to help his sister, who lived out of town, to organize his memorial service.

Through the memorial service, which was a beautiful coming together of the many aspects of Rob's life, I finally got to know who Rob was. I was awed, humbled and profoundly affected by this man and the way he lived his life. No one at the Retreats knew that Rob was a NASA scientist. Rob's life's work was all about making information accessible across disciplines on a global scale, so that separate groups of scientists might get a broader perspective of their individual and collective work. Rob addressed seminars of 15,000 scientists—in a *suit*, I might add; I saw the photos!

Despite the advanced technology used as part of his job, Rob neither owned a cell phone nor a car. He walked to work. His passion was Dances of Universal Peace, spiritual practice in motion. Rob would turn up anywhere at a moment's notice if there was a chance to teach this practice that was so close to his heart.

From the stories that were shared with me about Rob's kindness and compassion, his love of his niece and nephew and his delight in nature, Rob now appears before me as an example and a major life lesson. I did not learn this lesson at Retreat. I did not learn this lesson from spending time in his living friendship. I learned this lesson from his spirit, as carried by those who knew him. Rob lives more in me now than he ever did while he was alive. His lesson to me is to never overlook anyone. Everyone has something to teach us; everyone carries a part of the creative source of life; everyone has their own beauty.

In the words of one of Rob's favorite Sufi dances;

How could anyone ever tell you
You were anything less than beautiful?
How could anyone ever tell you
You were less than whole?
How could anyone fail to notice that your loving is a miracle?
How deeply you're connected to my soul.
(words and music by Alaskan singer/songwriter Libby Roderick)

I danced to this song at his memorial service. Bowing to another and looking into the windows of their soul, the words caused an overwhelming recognition in me of the love we all deserve and are here to give each other. There was no me and them, there was just love. My eyes blurred with tears as I made my way around the dance circle. How could I have thought of Rob as anything less than beautiful when his fondest wish was for us all to know our own beauty and interconnectedness?

After the service as refreshments were served, I sought out those I might have previously overlooked and found a poet, a musician, and an artist. I now look at everyone differently because of Rob. My heart is more open and my life is richer. Though Rob is gone in this physical plane, he is a part of everyone whose life he touched, and I'm so glad he touched mine. Rob is forever deeply connected to my soul.

Sisters of Mercy

By Tom Rebold

Several years ago during a sculpture class, I got stuck on a project where we had to use an entire brick of modeling clay. I'd made an interesting shape just squeezing stuff together, but there was still half the clay left and I didn't want to wreck what had taken me some time to create by sticking something else on it. The instructor came by and looked it over like he was sizing up a horse, "Try turning it over. Isn't that interesting?" Now my favorite part was concealed beneath it, and I had a new view of a part that was formerly ignored...hmmm. He laughed, "The best art often comes from accident."

To drive home his point, he went to his office and came back with a cartoon sketch of a bird in a cage. The bird looked forlorn and trapped; however, the cage was peculiar—it only had about six wires. He could have walked right out! I guessed the bird was a prisoner of habit. "See?" he said. "The cage is in our heads, and we can leave any time we want." I learned a lot in his class, but that first lesson was probably the most important.

Recently, my friend Shannon and I took a drive down to Monastery Beach, south of Carmel-by-the-Sea to enjoy some time off on our break from teaching. The beach forms a natural bowl framed by Point Lobos State Park and the Ribera peninsula, where the waves slosh up the steep sides before collapsing back into the sea. Across the road lies a mission-style monastery with a tall adobe steeple rising against the deep green of the Santa Lucia Mountains.

Something about its presence invited us to walk up the long road to gain a closer look at the buildings and the grounds surrounding it. We arrived at the main building, adjacent to the chapel, simply adorned with several large marble disks set above the covered walkway. A sign adjacent to a closed door explained that this was a working nunnery of the Carmelite Order and was not open for tourism, although the chapel hours indicated periods when it was open to the public. Since the chapel was currently locked, we began drifting back to the roadway. But as we approached the entrance we saw the gates closing before us.

It was 4:30, the posted closing time on the sign. The property was surrounded by a rusty looking chain-link fence, and there were no buttons to open the gate from the inside. We went back up to the closed door we had visited earlier and pressed the button on the intercom. A woman answered, explaining that the monastery was closed, but that we could just drive out through the gate. "But we came on foot!" we exclaimed. "Oh, I'm sorry, we're in the middle of something right now. You'll have to wait. Perhaps someone will be leaving at 5."

It seemed more than slightly surreal to be sitting outside on a bench, looking out at the sea, waiting for a nun who might decide to leave so we could get out. What if they forgot about us? Was the light starting to dim? Was the fog bank offshore moving in? We got up, restless, and began walking down to the fence. Could we scale it? "Not me," said Shannon, who was wearing large-toed boots. We went back to the gate—thick, black metal bars filled in with curly scroll work. Not really any convenient spot to gain purchase; plus if we were up there and the gate opened, it could get messy. That's when I saw something: the left gate had an eight-inch wide space between two bars. "Hey, we can just slip through the bars," I said, and before we could think of a reason why not, I climbed up and stepped over a nasty pointed thing, squeezed sideways, and turned my head 90 degrees over my left shoulder so it would fit. Shannon, who is even thinner than I (we both suffer from a kind of underweight syndrome,) hesitated, remembering a traumatic situation of being stuck in a tight place, but finally relented, seeing no other way out.

Outside at last, walking back to the car, a sudden euphoria

overtook us as we laughed at our unhealthy-looking thin-ness. "We passed through the eye of the needle!" I said, feeling something like a bird who had just escaped a cage. The situation seemed ripe with metaphorical connotations: sure, the nuns were doing their own valuable work and didn't want to be bothered with interlopers. But maybe a certain playful spirit had stepped in to show a couple of bound souls how easy it could be to free themselves.

It seems the feeling carried over into my larger life struggles because the very next day, while stretching, something popped in my back, releasing a year-old block that was interfering with my health. It was like a switch came on and suddenly things were working again. After many months obsessing over that problem from different angles, and agonizing over surgery and other unpleasant options, I wasn't expecting it to vanish that easily. The best answers are those that come by accident.

Control the Pain

By *Amy Lloyd*

There is a group of people who truly live in the moment, largely because they have no other choice. In the small fishing town of Phuket, Thailand lives the Moken tribe. These people find food in any way possible and can hold their breath underwater longer than other humans. Instead of working against their environment, they work with it, respecting nature and honoring the land. They also honor their life experience. If pain comes, they acknowledge it, living always present in the moment. I took this way of living to heart and vowed to apply it to my own life.

Eckhart Tolle, a Dutch spiritual teacher best known for *The Power of Now*, suggests real healing can only occur when we direct our thoughts right through the barrel of pain. Breathe it, speak it, and feel it till the moment it is done and moves out of us, like a parasite. I don't want to cheat myself out of the highs and lows and I don't want to look back on my life as a series of vague moments with no defined edges. But certainly no one likes to feel pain.

My father has been dealing with cancer for twenty-one years now. In spite of our incredibly fractured relationship, we have come together these last few years as his disease has progressed. I was not in denial of his condition nor was he. There was a particularly shattering day when I accompanied him and my mother to the cancer ward. He had become so fatigued from dehydration that it was critical to get him to an intravenous drip.

I sat with them both in the tiny cancer treatment room while they pumped saline into his veins. He moaned often and my mother wept in the chair, looking more like crumpled, unfolded laundry than a person. I wanted to run, to gallop the hell out of that horrible, stench-filled hospital and away from my writhing, dying father. And who would have blamed me? It was agonizing to watch my father dying. I could not bear it. But I could not bear to deny it either. A higher and deeper wisdom gently tugged at me to stay in that awful little room and keep my heart open. So I made the choice, the conscious choice to be present and witness to it all. In that moment I breathed into all that was transpiring and I kept myself accountable to my promise. Being here was not born out of pain; it was born out of love.

Life is lived from one end of the spectrum to the other, and here it all unfolded in front of me. The man who watched me be born I was now watching die: a spiritual passing of the baton. It was an honor to be there, taking in every drop of life left. The art of being present when everything human inside of us wishes to close down is the very act of love. Trust me—this I have learned.

I got dad to eat a small cardboard container of vanilla ice cream; his face was bloated, but his eyes filled with gratitude. It wasn't up to me to control his pain and it wasn't really even up to me to control mine. The thing to do was just be with it all. My gratitude for Spirit gifting me this experience is immeasurable. It birthed my heart anew and in better shape.

Several days later, Dad called. He thanked me for being with him.

"Amy, I was remembering the adventure we had in the cancer ward." Adventure! Even as a grown woman, I was moved by my father's very need to somehow make light of an event he would just as soon shield from his daughter's eyes.

"Of course, Dad," I replied, noticing the faintness, the weakness in his voice—the same voice that for most of my life could crush me with a scathing criticism.

"Well, what do you think we should put on our special wheelchair?" Always the writer, my father began to weave the fine fantastical details.

"What about a potato gun, or sirens?" I offered. He agreed

those would be nice additions. Turkey sandwiches, ice cream, of course, and a whistle were also included in our special transport. Finishing touches included an Indian chief hat and special wheels, so it could roll up flights of stairs.

"Where are we going on this magical wheelchair?"

Expecting him to say something like Treasure Island or Italy or an interstellar planet only special people know about, his response surprised me.

"To find the doctor who can fix me, of course." Of course!

Love, like pain, is not in the general—love is very specific. When you see someone's heart: the thumbprints, the caves and valleys, the tangles and threads—when you see the entirety of their richly complex soul, do not deny the experience. Instead take it in to the fullest part of you. Be a conscious witness. I cherish those last few years, months, and days more than you can imagine. It turns out that feeling the depth of pain is really feeling the height of love, and that realization came because I remained fully awake to life.

At the far end of a fully experienced experience is grace. I do believe that the depths match the heights and I would rather fly up in a magical wheelchair, bumps and bruises, eyes wide open, any day.

Shake

By Joan Doyle

I lie awake. The clock says 3:28. I have been shifting positions now for maybe a half hour in an attempt to relax and fall back to sleep, but it's not working. My shoulders are tense, my head shakes on my pillow; sleep will not come. I think about this tremor I have been experiencing in my head. I am not an old lady: my hands do not waver, my step is sure, but I have been experiencing a persistent head shake now for almost a year. I have been to doctors and I try to maintain a diet that was recommended to relieve the muscle tightness. No nightshade vegetables (potatoes, tomatoes, bell peppers), and of course, no sugar. I do my spiritual work, too. I affirm my unshakeable faith in Spirit to heal.

As I lie awake in the darkness I wonder if it is not the beginning of a progressive illness. I want it gone. It distracts me from so much. I am conscious of it at work, wondering if someone thinks I am saying no when I am agreeing with them. Sometimes I am aware it's happening especially in a seated position, during meditation, for example, or talking with a client. I tend to prefer to be alone so I don't have to wonder, am I shaking now, and what is this person thinking about it? I feel I am categorized as an object of pity, and if not, then that the person I am dealing with is distracted by it, having their own thoughts about it. Maybe they are thanking God they don't shake.

At times it feels as if I can control it if I remember to relax. Sometimes I think *I am steady today*, and my husband remarks on how my head really began to shake as I turned to look at something. I can't seem to forget it's there. I am tired of it. I don't want to have to fight it anymore.

As I turn once more in my bed, disturbing the cat at my feet, I think of how many other people out there are experiencing physical challenges so much worse than this one. I think of a conversation I had earlier, last evening, about how sometimes it's best to lean into what we are trying to push away. I wonder how I can lean into this, surrender to its message to me. I have asked if I am saying no to something, and I got the idea that I have often denied myself, not allowed myself to be me, holding a picture of what is expected or acceptable to be in the world, and attempting to be that instead. Be a good girl, be sensible; I suppose I have always been susceptible to what others think of me. I think, too, of how I have grown in compassion for others because of dealing with this.

Accepting it and not pushing it away feels like a softer and gentler path. My heart softens toward myself, and at the same time to the infirmities of the elderly. They are me and I am them. As a spiritual being I cannot separate myself from others, and as a human being, I am heir to all that living in a body means. I feel more connected with the human race when I don't impose an idea of perfection on myself or anyone else. These ideas float around in my head as I struggle to sleep. I think about tomorrow and how tired I will be. Yet there is nothing for it but to rise and write this down.

As I wait for the computer to boot up, I make some chamomile tea. My cat ambles out from the bedroom to keep me company. She looks up into my face after she has settled herself on my lap. I have no idea what she is thinking, but I am grateful for her company. I know one thing, she is not thinking about my head shaking and I love her for that.

The Journey

By Justin Elledge

The pain abated as the Novocain took effect, and the fire in my mouth quickly subsided bringing a tear to my eye; the joy of peace returned. How little did I realize that a simple root canal would forever change my life and the path I was on. That was October 1985.

For three days the antibiotics were taken faithfully to follow up on the doctor's direction, and I thought my life would return to its current rhythm of work, weekends and fun in-between. However, on the fifth day I felt what I can only describe as a hollowness or vague emptiness come over me. It was nothing I could put my finger on, but I began to feel myself slip away, losing weight, ounce by ounce, and day by day.

I was not worried at first, as I called the dentist a few weeks after the root canal and he assured me there could be no connection between the two; and making the mistake of believing him, I began my descent into the journey of the Wounded Healer.

In 1985 I had weighed 220 and by May of 1986, I was down sixty pounds, hitting my lowest at 160. From what little health insurance I had, I went from doctor to doctor to no avail. Each time I would tell them that it had all started with having had a root canal, to which they would politely nod, and in disbelief they would dismiss it as a causal agent.

All the tests came back negative for any of the known issues such as AIDS, Crohn's disease, hepatitis, and cancer. In fact my "bloodwork" was some of the best they had seen—my cholesterol once getting as low as 135. I was eventually diagnosed as having Malabsorption Syndrome and I was prescribed enzymes for it; however I never did gain the weight back, and in my heart, I knew the diagnosis was indeed, wrong.

So began my journey away from allopathic medicine, and I started down that path, turning to others outside of the healthcare field. I began by consulting nutritionists, chiropractors, allergists, and tried their programs, but none of them worked. They all agreed it was a mystery. The only thing I was sure of was that I wasn't getting any richer.

In frustration, I also began seeking out psychics and others who had begun their own journey to better health and enlightenment. Some had keen insights to my life, and others did not, however they encouraged me to continue looking for an answer.

My then girlfriend encouraged the use of my hands for something other than woodwork, and suggested becoming a massage therapist. It was then that the first door opened to my second sight. In those few early days of exploration in massage school, a new world opened up to me as I placed hands upon others and images from their lives began to flood into my mind. At the end of the week, every other student was lining up for me to work on them, and often I would see them fade into unconsciousness as Spirit worked through me.

During the class, the instructor pulled me aside and asked me how long I had been working as a massage therapist, and I said, "Oh, about five days." She looked at me surprised, saying, "I have been teaching this for over 20 years, and those who have reached your level of mastery and understanding with clients is unheard of. I have seen others, who have spent a lifetime performing massage, but only rarely have I met anyone who can do what you are doing, and you are a novice! Do you have any idea how rare your ability is?" I had no idea. I thought everyone doing massage saw their client's life issues pass before them.

A few more years passed and my health had reached a state of equilibrium, or perhaps stalemate. Not getting better, or worse. During the 90's I became a vocational nurse, married and divorced, put my massage training behind me, and eventually settled into a life of design and engineering.

In 2002 I again found myself feeling melancholy; my spirit felt tired and I needed to find that inner path again. Inspired, I went to a retreat in Julian, California, high in mountains and far from my life as I could get. These retreats were based on "A Course in Miracles," and opened a door to meditation and camaraderie that I had been hungering for my entire life. For the first time, among these newfound friends, I finally felt at home. Returning to the retreats again and again over the years brought me to a better understanding, through prayer and meditation, of who I was and why I am here.

During a retreat over Easter Sunday in 2005, a doorway opened again, and I never looked back. For me, that event was truly a time of life, death and resurrection. During the retreat, I was called to do some energy work on a friend to relieve some pain I thought was in his neck and shoulders. I knelt down next to him on the floor, and I held my hands above his chest for only a few seconds when an image of a bloody broken rib on the right side of his chest appeared to me. Asking him to show me exactly where it was he was feeling the most pain, with his right hand he pointed to a spot on his right lower chest. I then said to him, "You, my friend, have a broken rib." Almost in denial my friend said, "I was afraid of that." And the room went quiet. X-rays confirmed the break a few days later.

The next day, Easter Sunday, Jim, a musician, was complaining about some pain in his wrist. As he did so, an image of scar tissue in his neck from a prior surgery appeared to me. The vision showed that scar tissue from a prior surgery on his neck was giving him the feeling of pain in his wrist. And that the wrist pain was only a symptom. I mentioned this to him and he said "You know, Justin, it's funny you should say that. That was the same thing my doctor told me." I was in shock.

This ability continued manifesting with many others, almost everywhere I went in the weeks and months to follow. I was highly encouraged to use this gift and to help others. This journey has yet to reach its end. I know that everything I have learned and experienced—the pain, the anguish, the compassion and determination, and also joy to carry on has given me a strength I have yet to fully understand.

The Get-Out-of-Jail-Free Card

By Joan Doyle

I felt dead inside. I was a zombie, walking slowly through the routines of my life. I was able to work. I was able to eat, though without much pleasure. Everything good had already happened in my life. I couldn't envision a thing for my future—I knew I was depressed.

I was depressed because I had just called off my engagement to a good man. I felt I had destroyed his happiness; and for what—this? My life was not worth living; I could find no joy. I was a baggage he might as well have, though I don't know why he would want me. The frustrating thing was my body was healthy. I wanted to lie down and die. I imagined doing just that; laying myself out in my best dress and make-up, and waiting for death to take me. I knew it was ridiculous. I had no protégé like Mrs. Havisham, nor did I have her vitriol to poison another being with hatred, nothing to keep me occupied in my bitter days. I had been the one who left the other person in the lurch, so all I was left with was guilt. It is not a motivating emotion, unlike Mrs. Havisham's desire for revenge.

I lived in bleak house, and yet somewhere within me there was a spark, a tiny point of light. I was waiting; waiting for that ember to ignite again. I read somewhere that even in times of depression when it seems nothing is happening on the surface, everything is rearranging itself on a deeper level; a new structure of beliefs is being formed. This must have been the case with me.

A good friend asked if I would like to create a vision board collage. She said it would be a good thing for me, so that I might begin to create my life anew. I was grateful for her friendship and so I agreed. We got together at her beautiful home, and spent the afternoon drinking tea and cutting out images from magazines. It was as if I was making the collage for someone other than myself. I cut pictures out, of traveling, as it was something I had always enjoyed. "She might like this, as she did enjoy it before," I would think to myself. "And she always liked daffodils; they are a sign of spring. That works, don't you think—renewal after the winter?" I picked a photo of a happy person walking across a bridge. I picked positive words like love, joy, friendship.

I came across a word in big orange capitals and stuck it right in the middle—GRACE. I knew grace was a gift, something freely given that you didn't have to do anything to deserve. Like a *Get out of jail free* card. I felt at that time I didn't deserve all the things I was placing on my vision board, but that by God's grace I might one day find enthusiasm for life again.

And it came to pass, as they like to say in the Gospels, that Joan did return to the land of the living. It took a little time, but slowly joy crept in and that point of light began to glow again. Looking back, I'm grateful for all of it. I have grown in compassion for other's painful choices. I have grown in trust in myself, for my decision was correct, and I have grown in faith in the process of life. I cannot always see what is to come but I trust all is unfolding as it should. Today I love my life, but I know if one day it doesn't look as I would like, that my Spirit is strong and with the grace of God I will endure.

A Different Journey

By Sandi Duncan

Two weeks before I got the news no one wants to hear I already had a premonition of things to come. It happened during my morning meditation as I was praying for "right employment" —a message so loud and clear it was as if I'd heard the voice of God whispering in my ear saying, "You don't need to look for work right now. You are going on a different journey; you'll be walking a different path now." That was it. No further illumination on what that journey was to be, just those ominous words that echoed in my brain. Coming out of that meditation, I felt unsettled, almost unnerved, and told my partner I was worried. I've often gotten messages from spirit in my meditations but this one was different.

The call came two weeks later at 8:00 am on Thursday, May 11, 2006. It was my doctor informing me I had ovarian cancer. I'd tell you I was surprised and shocked, but the truth was when I heard those words they were exactly what I thought I'd hear. Between the message I got from spirit and the medical tests I'd had two days prior, I had a very clear idea that things were indeed going to be different.

On those first difficult days after learning I had cancer, my mind was not functioning in a logical or rational manner. Rather than being concerned that I had a life-threatening illness, I was worrying about how I was going to pay for treatment, since I had no health insurance at the time of my diagnosis. As I've found so many times in my life, the universe conspires in unforeseen and often magical ways to give us the perfect answers and solutions to our life challenges when we let go and let God.

The "divine" resolution to my financial challenge came three days after that fateful call. I had already spent a horrific 20 hours in a county hospital ER only to be turned away because there were no beds. I could find no human answer for my situation so I put it in the hands of God. On Sunday, May 14th at 1:50 pm my friend Wendy called informing me that another friend's father, a gynecological oncologist, was giving a lecture at 2:00 pm at a location ten minutes from me and she barked an order to "GO!" I did. That call and my willingness to "GO" ultimately led me to the man who literally saved my life.

The following afternoon I found myself in the office of a doctor who agreed to operate on me despite my lack of health insurance. And this human angel went so much further than that. Not only did he provide the medical care I needed, he arranged for all the financial challenges to be handled in a way that got me the treatment I needed before it was too late. The resolution to my health and financial problems proved divine providence at work.

With the financial aspect solved I began my journey into a world that was as foreign to me as if I'd landed on Mars. It was the world of doctors and hospitals, surgeries and medications: things that made me feel as awful as a human being can feel, all to save my life. And...it worked. It was truly a different path to walk than *my* world which, until that point, had not consisted of the world of western medicine but rather of integrative healing and spiritual practices. It was a time in my life where I had to let go and let others be the caregivers—something I had a challenge doing as I've been a holistic healthcare practitioner for years and it was my job to take care of others. I had to give others the opportunity to be there for me and it was harder than I could imagine. Fortunately, I'm abundantly blessed with a loving community of friends and family who were there for me every step of the way. Between my family and friends and this amazing doctor, my life was saved by a community of human angels.

Despite finding myself in the alien world of bright lights and sterile equipment, unpleasant smells and invasions of my body, I did take care of my "wellness" throughout the eight months of surgeries and chemo. Because of my spiritual foundation and my practice as a holistic healthcare practitioner, I was well equipped to walk that companion road to cancer treatment. I used my aromatherapy, meditation, drumming and energy healing practices to carry me through one of the darkest times of my life, and it made the journey lighter and the road easier to walk.

The story doesn't end there. This journey certainly put me on a different path in all ways—body, mind and spirit, and it challenged me on all levels. During the long months of treatment and recovery I found it nearly impossible to meditate; the chemo fogged my brain and made focusing on anything a near Herculean task. I was exhausted all the time and some days I felt like I was sleepwalking through mud. Everything was difficult. I could no longer identify myself, but through it all my will to live was strong and I never entertained the thought that I might die.

Toward the end of my treatment, I was meditating through my fog and asked, "What is the major lesson you want me to walk away with from this experience?" Just as this journey had begun with a whispering from spirit, the message immediately came to me: "It's all about balance—body, mind and spirit. You left out one-third of that equation: your body. You also needed to see that people working in Western Medicine are as dedicated to healing people as you are. How can you do healing work and help those in need if you won't set foot in a hospital environment? We needed you to see that healing is about integrating Western Medicine with spirituality and holistic healing. It's about balance."

I got that message loud and clear. Today I'm healthier in body, mind and spirit than I've ever been in my life. I take advantage of all the tools at my disposal to maintain my wellness, and as I write this, I've been in remission from advanced ovarian cancer for over six years.

The Wisdom of the Blue Sapphire

By Joan Doyle

Reluctantly I got out of the taxi. The driver had no English whatsoever and I had no Thai. My map was Greek to him. Bleary-eyed, there was nothing for it but to walk to the Central Post Office, where the public phones were located, and wait for it to open. Then I could begin the task of setting things right.

The day before was my first day in Thailand and what began as a grand adventure had gone terribly wrong, without me suspecting a thing. I had never traveled alone in an exotic Asian city before, so exiting at Hualampong train station, my senses were thoroughly assaulted. Throngs of scooters, tuc-tuc taxis and bicycles packed high with boxes careened by, while chickens pecked the pavement underfoot. Honking horns, exhaust fumes and strong odors added to the chaos. I couldn't see a single street signs to help me navigate to the temple of the world's largest golden Buddha, Wat Traimit, that was to be my first stop. When I did make it to the temple I had to take a long breather to recover my equilibrium. Why had I felt the need to do this alone?

I would not be deterred, however. The next stop was the Grand Palace. Would I trust a driver to take me there? The guide book said to be wary as you might be persuaded to take a side trip to the driver's brother's trinket store. It was too far to walk so I hailed a tuc-tuc, and true to form, the driver asked if it was ok if we took a detour from our route to stop for gas. I said no, and with some trepidation I asked him to let me out where we were. Continuing on foot, not sure of the scale of my map, I felt lost and tense and I was suspicious of everyone even as I asked directions.

Finally, overheated and still on edge, I got to within a stone's throw of the golden-turreted Grand Palace, and I stopped to drink some water and rest at a pretty shrine draped with orchids and jasmine. A nicely dressed man with excellent English struck up a conversation with me where I sat. I could feel myself relaxing as we chatted. He enquired about my plans for the day. I was hoping to visit a few more temples after seeing the Grand Palace. To my great dismay he told me the palace was closed; it was the Queen's birthday. He went on to say that as a very special gift to the Thai people, the Royal Lapidary was opened up for viewing. There I would see how stones were mined, cut and made into beautiful jewelry. Thailand was known for its rubies and sapphires. Americans are their best customers, reselling gems for twice the price back home, he confided. He affably suggested he could get me a good fare with a tuc-tuc driver to take me to the Royal Lapidary. As I tell this tale to you it seems like such an obvious setup, but this neophyte never questioned it.

I went to the Lapidary, watched the movie, drank their iced orange juice and perused their beautiful jewelry with a firm resolve to resist purchasing anything. But lo and behold, I left the establishment with a $400 sapphire ring, in the bus they provided on my way to the Thai dance performance and dinner location they recommended. They were full of smiles and I was pretty happy with myself.

It seemed like the perfect ending to my day as I ate my dinner alone and watched the petite, ornately dressed ladies with the pointed fingers move gracefully in synch. Perfect, that is, until I read in my guide book that gem fraud is rife in Bangkok, that there is a division of the Police devoted to dealing with it alone. *"Never,"* the book said, *"go to a gem dealer recommended by a man who approaches you on the street speaking perfect English!!"* My mind was set into a tail spin.

On returning to the hotel that evening I wondered how I had missed the huge posters, now apparently everywhere, saying, "If you believe you have been a victim of gem fraud, call this number." As the bed sheets knotted around me in the wee small hours, I vowed to protest outside the Royal Lapidary warning people to beware. I was angry at myself for succumbing to the ruse. I felt stupid, gullible and could not believe I had spent so much money. I had one more day in Bangkok—would I get to any of the sights at all?

Already exhausted on reaching the post office, the frustration of coins and foreign phones (not to mention calling police offices that passed me along or left me hanging on the line) wore me to a frazzle. Finally I stepped outside, and finding a stone bench in the shade of a tree, I took out the sapphire ring. I tried it on. It was a beautiful thing even if it was a fake; friends back home would never know; maybe this was a lesson in the value of things. Value is all about perception, it seems. I had believed it was real, but this was an expensive lesson.

It was approaching noon and I felt as if I had not done a thing I had dreamed about for months prior to the trip. I made the decision then it was time to just let go of the whole ring affair, to keep the ring as a reminder to myself to be more cautious in future. No longer in fight mode I felt a weight come off my shoulders. With a resolve to enjoy the day and with a new spring in my step I began to stride off in the direction of the Grand Palace.

I had not gone fifty yards when I saw a booth which said Tourist Police. I hesitated before deciding to approach the window. What had I got to lose at this point? Within two minutes I found myself holding on to my hat as a police officer whisked me across Bangkok on the back of his motorcycle. Within an hour I had my money in my pocket and I was back on the street.

I had the bizarre feeling I had been reborn. I suddenly knew exactly how to deal with the locals. When my next taxi driver delivered me to a closed side-gate of the palace, telling me it was closed and asking if I'd like to see the reclining Buddha several miles out of town, I said thank you very much, no, and stepped out. When he asked for four baht for the ride, I gave him two which is what it was worth. As for the Palace, it was magnificent and I thoroughly enjoyed the rest of my day, which included a Thai massage and some of the most enormous Buddha statues I had ever seen.

My experience transformed the moment I let go—the frustration, the striving, the anger at myself only served to make me feel like a victim, powerless and stuck. Accepting things as they were, looking for the lessons to take forward, and then focusing on what I knew I would enjoy brought me back into the flow of life. From this place everything came right, easily and effortlessly. Life can work this way. We cannot change the wind they say but we can adjust the sail. Life wants to be lived through us joyously, I have come to believe, and I try to move quickly toward letting go whenever frustration, anger or resentment show up. It's a bit of work, but it never fails to enhance my life experience.

I may have left my sparkling blue sapphire behind in Thailand, but I came away with something much more valuable: a priceless gem of wisdom and that I will never trade.

Synchronicity

For the sense of being which in calm hours rises,
we know not how, in the soul, is not diverse from things,
from space, from light, from time, from man,
but one with them and proceeds obviously from the same source whence their
life and being also proceeds.
- Emerson

Synchronicity was coined by Carl Jung to describe a *significant coincidence* of physical and psychological phenomena that have no cause to be connected. That is, they *seem* to have no cause to be connected except that everything is connected in the One Energy from which everything in the universe has emanated. When we witness a synchronicity, it means we are in synch, connected with the One Eternal and limitless Energy. The message we are being given, about the direction we are moving in, is one of affirmation. When we acknowledge synchronicities, which happen spontaneously and without effort, we acknowledge our unifying consciousness. Thus Spirit is reminding us we are limitless souls, not alone, not separate, but always connected.

Little Miracles Everywhere

By Joan Doyle

Justin called from Las Vegas to say he had arrived and found the Temple. My mind saw flashing neon and golden Buddhas, burning incense and slot machines. *I suppose it's a place that needs a temple more than most*, I thought, as he tried to describe to me the Buddha enlivening ceremony of which he was to be a part.

"I have been asked to blow the Tibetan Long Horn," he told me, admitting he was a little intimidated by the prospect, as he had never done it before.

"Oh, you'll be great," I reassured him, with the love that saw his potential to do anything he set his mind to do, even as I was unsure what a Tibetan Long Horn was.

"I wish you were here," he whispered.

"I look forward to your return," I said, my heart so full with love it felt like it would burst. Just three short months since we started dating, but I knew this man was very special and this relationship was significant.

"I look forward to meeting your brother," he said.

"Come by the house on your way home, if it's not too late and you're not too tired," I invited, before we said our goodnights.

The next afternoon I picked my brother up at the airport with mounting excitement. The prospect of sharing my alternate universe with a family member in person was almost more than I could stand. He would get to experience palm trees and sunshine and multilane freeways and the myriad contrasts to our native home of green and wet Ireland, in real time. I could never describe this. It was like a cat trying to explain to a fish what it was like to live out of water. On top of that I wanted him to meet Justin, the person who was amazing me daily.

I was jumping out of my skin with excitement and pleasure as I waffled to him of my plans for his stay and the things we would do. He grinned and took in his surroundings, and I knew for him this was a dream come true. Thirteen years I had been living in Los Angeles, and on more than thirteen visits back home I'd brought back tales of my adventures, as I kept up with my large and expanding family. I wished I could share more of my life with them, but the two places being so culturally and climatically opposite, it was difficult for them to relate, if they had never been here. Now I would not feel so alone in my experiences.

"Today," I said, "we will take it easy. Once you are settled I'll take you out around the neighborhood so you can get your bearings. It will help you cope with the time-zone change to get some sunlight and a little exercise."

"I can't wait," he laughed. "Whatever we do will be great. I do have one request, though, and you can probably imagine what that is."

"To go fishing!" I easily guessed, as my brother Jody is a fanatical fisherman.

"Yes, and when will I get to meet this new man of yours, Mr. Just In Time! I have to vet him on behalf of the family, you know."

"Hopefully, tomorrow night, he will be back from Vegas but he may be tired. If not tomorrow, then the next night; we can go to dinner."

The next day being a Sunday, Jody accompanied me to experience my church and we had lunch with some of my friends. From there we headed for Santa Monica, on the way stopping by Melrose Market. We share a love of antiques and eclectic objet d'art, as well as bargains, so this was a real treat. As I browsed in the busy chaos and the bustle, I spotted some silver jewelry. I tried on a couple of pieces and fell in love with a broad silver ring with Sanskrit symbols in relief. It was adjustable, and fully closed it fit my middle finger. It occurred to me to buy it for Justin, but I dismissed the idea. Three months and I'm buying him rings! Too soon! I moved on but I couldn't stop thinking about the ring. When it was time to leave, I felt I couldn't leave the ring behind. I retraced my steps and thought, "If it's not gone already I will buy it." I bought it and I wore it, unsure if it was for Justin or for me.

Jody and I had a fabulous day. The highlight for him was chatting with fishermen on Santa Monica Pier, talking of fish that got away and those that were eaten with relish. It was getting late when we finally made it home. Justin had left a message to say he was an hour from Los Angeles and was hoping to call by. After the sea air, Jody felt it would be best if he met Justin the next evening, as he was exhausted. I wished him a good night's sleep.

I made some tea for myself and put on some soft music. The balmy September evening was filled with the scent of orange blossoms, and it wafted in the open door as I sat in anticipation of Justin's arrival. I didn't have to wait long. We sat on the couch holding hands and sharing the events of our short separation in low tones, so as not to keep Jody awake. Eventually I said, "I have something for you." Only in that moment did I know for sure that the ring was for him.

"You do?" Justin inquired.

"Yes, and it's already in your hand," I said.

He looked down at my hand in his, and I pulled the ring off my finger.

"This is for you," I said timidly, yet with certainty.

"It is?" Justin smiled as he examined it in surprise. "What does it say?"

"It says Om Mani Padme Hum; it's Sanskrit, a mantra of compassion," I explained.

His eyes widened.

"I have something for you too," he exclaimed excitedly and jumped to his feet. He reached in his pocket and he pulled out a rectangular silver pendant.

"You won't believe it," his face was beaming as he handed it to me.

"I won't believe what?" I asked.

"It says Om Mani Padme Hum, too."

We looked at each other in awe and delight—more synchronicity.

It seemed our early relationship was a series of synchronistic events just like this one. Everywhere we went there were signs and co-incidences. I cannot explain how or why, except to say it felt good, as if somehow our coming together was aligned with life's flow. I had never experienced anything like it before in my life. Little miracles everywhere; we see them still.

Living in Sync with My Soul

By Barbara Schiffman

Life is an unfolding series of synchronicities; in fact, *"Synchronicity is an ever present reality for those who have eyes to see,"* according to Swiss psychologist Carl Jung.

The events moving us from birth to death are most easily seen in hindsight. Looking back from the vantage point of sixty-plus years, this is certainly the case for me. But as I get older— and hopefully wiser—I'm seeing synchronicities far more clearly as my Soul's path is unfolding in front of me. I also listen better to my inner voice, which is my Soul speaking to and through me. So, synchronicity is an ever-present reality as I consciously "live in sync with my Soul."

The choices I make, the actions I take, and the people I encounter all shape my Soul's journey. I truly feel this life is the evolution of previous lifetimes as well as the "seed" for lives still to come. As I sense my Soul speaking to and through me, it often feels as if I'm living in stereo. The human part of me may think I'm "making it up," but my Soul helps me take action despite human resistance. So progress occurs, both inside and out.

After living in L.A. for five years, I synchronistically met my husband, Glenn, when I took a new job after splitting up with a guy who was not ready for a long-term relationship with me. Glenn had just returned from a year in Oregon building a house for a friend. On the day of my interview he was using a spare office in the Sunset Boulevard suite of the music manager who hired me. Glenn had previously worked as a rock 'n roll roadie and road manager, and was then writing a fictionalized memoir based on his wild experiences. Though I took the job to distract me from my broken heart, it only lasted three months. When I left the job, I kept Glenn, who had moved in with me a week after we met. As writers, we bonded quickly through our mutual appreciation of good storytelling and our compatible views of life as a series of interconnected events or "themes." Thirty-five years later, our blended plotline is still unfolding.

For the past dozen years, synchronicities have been frequent and show no signs of slowing down. After my parents became ill in 1999 and I became "my parents' parent," my spiritual life demanded attention as personal challenges overshadowed my Hollywood career. A flyer at the Bodhi Tree Bookstore about Inner Guide Meditation led me to get trained in this Jungian-inspired, "inner coaching" meditation process. It blends Tarot and Astrological archetypes to create energy shifts, transforming me and activating my Inner Teacher, which has since taken center-stage.

Writing, teaching and counseling are now focal points of my life. Each relationship, experience and event shapes me. My belief that our lives are stories in the Mind of God drew me to work with the Akashic Records—the spiritual dimension of our Souls' journeys through all lifetimes—and catapulted me into new levels of synchronistic "seeing."

In 2005, I was trained in a prayer process to access the Records, but it wasn't the right "key" for me. My spiritual path detoured through Integrated Energy Therapy, Hypnotherapy and Past Life Regression until, in August 2009, a "thought" popped into my head that was definitely Spirit speaking: "Look into the Akashic Records again. Find a new teacher." Before I could take action, I got an email that Linda Howe's new book, *How to Read the Akashic Records,* was on sale! I, of course, bought it and then learned Linda would teach her first Advanced Akashic Teachers Training in 2010. After we connected, I decided to commit to the training though I had no clue where the time or money would come from. But within four months, my work, income and family obligations all shifted to support me in becoming an Akashic Records Teacher. I now love teaching people "the language of their Soul" so they can listen when Spirit Talks.

As I live in synch with my Soul, I know all is well. We are all connected at the energetic and evolutionary level, and we are all expressing Spirit wherever we are!

A Joyful Visitation

By Joseph Doyle

I must reveal a strange event that happened on the Sunday evening of our family reunion and celebration of my father's anniversary mass. It was two years since his passing. As I was in the process of tending to my 91 year-old mother near her bedtime, I heard the radio murmuring on a low tone. I promptly turned it up and what I heard lit me up inside. It was Johnny Barry playing Dad's favorite tunes on local Carlow Radio. I was filled with joy, and a tear came to my eye to hear the familiar tone. I had not heard this program in the last two years. "Very strange," I thought to myself. "Da, you did it again!" At the back of my mind I could hear Dad singing along from his bedroom, as I used to hear him. His spirit had returned to celebrate his anniversary.

I was delighted with this, as I didn't know the exact setting on the dial for Johnny Barry's show on what is, and has been, part of the furniture for many, many years—the electric radio on top of the microwave. I have no idea who set it to that place or why it was even turned on, as low as it was. I turned it up even more to make sure my mother could hear it. She loved listening to his unique selection as dear old Dad had—propped up, probably finishing the Irish Independent crossword, with his bifocals resting on the end of his nose as he waited for dreamland slumber in his twilight years.

Love Has No Borders

By Laurie St. Clare

It had been six months since my mom died. Even though we had never had the greatest relationship, there were days I deeply missed her. I walked into my office at home and looked around at all the things that had been piling up—time to get cleaning. I turned on my computer and opened my iTunes for some music. I hadn't opened this program since my mom's memorial service. One of the things we both loved was music—and all sorts of it. I had put together a playlist of her favorite music to play with photos from her life in the room we had set up at her memorial. I was proud and impressed that her tastes ran from Billie Holiday to Guns N Roses.

It was with a heavy heart I turned on my iTunes and picked out some music to encourage a clean sweep of my office. Still, I was feeling melancholy. I walked to the window where the sun shone brightly. As I stood there, I picked up a gift my mother had given me. This gift was unusual because it was something she had bought retail and while traveling, neither of which she did frequently. She was an antique dealer so nearly all my gifts from her were antiques.

I held this Raku pottery heart in my hand. It was a rattle. I loved this gift. I loved the way it felt in my hand. It was plump and full, not exactly smooth but not rough either. It was blue and purple with shifting shades of grey and magenta. It had black Japanese writing on it. I ran my fingers over the writing as I stood looking outside into the sun as the music played. I shook the heart with all the pieces inside rattling around. I turned it over and to my surprise, at the very base of the heart was written in plain English BELIEVE.

How had I missed that all these years? I must have had it for at least four years now! I read the word again. As I re-read "Believe," the music changed, catching my attention. I turned, puzzled, knowing I had not selected Elton John, yet I recognized the beginning of the song but could not place it. I walked to my computer. There at the top of the screen read the single word BELIEVE. I was stunned. It was Elton John's song "Believe" that my iTunes had started to play.

I cried with happiness as this familiar song played, with its most beautiful lyrics bringing even more meaning into my life and "rattling" my heart. I listened intently to the message of belief in love because it's all we have, that love has no boundaries and no borders to cross. I knew this to be true without a doubt. It left me with a phrase repeating in my head and in my heart—*I believe in love, I believe in love, I believe in love...*

Message Received

By Gertrude Anne Doyle

I awoke one Sunday morning in the summer of 1995 with vivid images of a nightmare. I had dreamt that my friend Lena was dying and was calling out my name. I awoke and remembered that my friend Lena was calling out my name. In the dream her husband Gavin had died and she had no-one but me to call on for help.

Lena, an artist, and her husband, Gavin, had moved from London to Ireland in 1986. They pursued their dream of living independently in a farmhouse in the Kilkenny countryside, raising crops and keeping livestock and poultry. They aspired to live by the principles of John Seymour, and by his philosophy of self-sufficiency. It was through our shared interests in art and self-sufficiency, in our dream of living "the good life," that Lena and I became firm friends.

After the birth of my daughter I moved forty miles away with my partner to where I now live. In the following few years, a time of snail mail, pre-internet and mobile phones, we almost lost contact. Lena and Gavin had no phone but we kept in touch by visiting at Christmas and sometimes in the summer. Gavin was no longer the enthusiastic small holder he had once been; he was losing interest.

On that summer Sunday the nightmare played on my mind, and in the afternoon I decided to pay Lena a visit. I strapped my daughter into her baby seat and drove to Kilkenny; I reached Lena's house around 4 pm.

I saw a packed suitcase inside the door. Lena's table was set with a meal for one—she was alone and I knew something was up. Lena was a creature of habit. She suffered from a stomach condition requiring her to eat at regular hours; 9am, 1pm and 6pm. I had never known her to deviate from this. When I returned from extricating my daughter from the car, Lena cleared the table, made tea and revealed that she had been planning to catch a bus to Carlow town and telephone me from there in the hope that I could pick her up and take her home with me for a few days. Gavin had fled with their car the night before to catch the morning Rosslare-to-Pembroke car ferry between Ireland and Britain, and when Lena refused to go too, he left her to fend for herself.

Gavin had been drinking in a local pub and been taunted because of his English accent. Normally gentle and mild Gavin had been drawn into a heated political argument and his life had been threatened. On 31 August 1994, the IRA had declared a ceasefire in Northern Ireland; this marked an effective end to political violence in what was known as "The Troubles," but anti-British feelings had no ceasefire. If a scapegoat was to be found, then Gavin, with his cockney accent, could be a target for unscrupulous "Brits Out" republicans "settling old scores." Gavin had taken his death threat seriously, and terrified, had run for his life! Lena, also in fear, had thought of me.

I awoke one Sunday morning in the summer of 1995 with vivid images of a nightmare. I awoke and remembered that my friend Lena was calling out my name.

An Irish Connection

By Robert Duffy

Long, long ago there was a map of Ireland on my classroom wall. I was aged about six and was in Senior Infants, probably First Grade in the American system. Dublin, Cork and Galway were places I had heard of but there was also a constellation of other towns marked on the map. My village, Hacketstown, wasn't shown but there were places like Athlone, Drogheda, Castlebar, and Wexford, to name a few that might be vaguely familiar to American readers. However, Robert zoomed in on Ballinasloe, a town about a hundred miles away.

Ballinasloe...I wanted to go to Ballinasloe, nowhere else—Ballinasloe was my Shangri La. When preparing this wee story I Googled a map of the USA to see if I could give an American parallel for what I was feeling. Imagine your eye landing on Fort Wayne, Indiana; the whole country is there for you, but the only place you want to go is Fort Wayne, Indiana. (Sorry, Fort Wayne readers. Bear with me.)

When I was aged eleven, my father took my brother and me on a fishing trip to the west of Ireland. I remembered that my private excitement was all about Ballinasloe—we were going to pass through Ballinasloe. The fact that we were going to a huge lake with a castle on its shores didn't matter. For me it was all about—passing...through...Ballinasloe. However, we crossed the River Shannon and turned north, fifteen miles shy of my ambition. But there was enough happening with the fishing trip; my encounter with Ballinasloe would have to wait until I was older.

I first glimpsed the town when I was fourteen. A train took a bunch of us to an Irish language summer school on the far western seaboard of Connemara. I drooled when the train stopped at Ballinasloe station, and I could savour the housing estates nearby, and two church steeples on gently rising ground in the distance.

In time, I finished my secondary schooling and moved on to study in University College, Dublin, an experience I shared with people from all over Ireland and further afield. It was a mix, a hum, an adventure. While I was there I met Audrey and we fell in love. We married in her home town and moved back to my home town. We have three lovely children—but they are not children any more. Within the last twelve months, two grandchildren have added their magic to our lives.

Years ago, when I looked at that map on the wall, when I looked at Ballinasloe through the window of a parked train, I didn't know that my heart was already there. I didn't know that one of the churches I was looking at was where I would be married. Audrey was already there, playing on her avenue, living her life, beginning a journey that would take her to college in Dublin where she would encounter a fellow from a village that wasn't marked on any schoolroom map.

We are still living happily ever after.

Dreams
and Visions

It is through your own soul that the voice of God speaks to you.
This is the interior guide.
- Emerson

The chaotic content of our dreams can often be a result of a stressful day, but occasionally we remember a dream that has a message of illumination on some aspect of our lives. Freud called dreams the royal road to the unconscious. Dreams can also connect us to the collective unconscious, as we transcend the boundaries of our bodies. They are a rich source of connection with divine wisdom and inspiration, and if we bring our attention to them, they too, can be a guiding light on our path to the understanding of ourselves and the world we live in.

Some people don't need to be in a dream state to sense the presence of incorporeal beings; they have no barriers to other dimensions and see visions while awake.

If dreams are something that fascinate you, try keeping a dream journal by your bed. This is telling your subconscious that you are ready to interpret its message. Remember the symbols in your dreams are unique to you. Take note of the emotions that are evoked, how do they reflect some situation you are facing in your waking life? It is often as we retell the dream or write it down that the sense is revealed. If you have a question to which you would like an answer, write it in your journal as you nod off at night. Write your dream instantly on awakening because it will often disappear as you become conscious.

Bob's Gift

By Joan Doyle

As the Lord's Prayer is recited in varied tones around me I close my eyes. The murmur lulls me, and in my mind's eye I see the stained-glass windows of my hometown church back in Ireland. I look sideways along the varnished wooden pew and there my mother is seated with her glasses perched on the end of her nose. Next to her stands my father in a familiar green wool jumper; he nods to me as the prayer ends and my brothers kneel down. I open my eyes and I am returned to the tanned faces of my colorful California church community. "Everyone we encounter has a message or lesson for us," the minister is saying. "It's easiest to just accept that and receive the gift. Sometimes the gifts are like Christmas and a birthday all at once and sometimes they are a lot less welcome." As always I can relate to what he is saying; I have known both painful lessons and sweet—all gifts, in hindsight, which have shaped me into who I am today. One deeply satisfying gift I received lately comes to mind. It took the form of a story which I will retell here to pay it forward.

My friend Bob, had a dream one night not long after his wife's father, George, passed away. In the dream his father-in-law appeared to him as he did while alive and told him that all was well with him. This is not an unusual dream to have. I have had at least two such dreams. The first happened the night after my friend was killed in a motorcycle accident. He appeared in a dream sitting on the side of my bed, where I slept. He stroked my head and whispered, "It's ok you know, it's ok."

The second occurred some months after my father died. I had a dream that I was in my mother's house with some of my siblings, and there in the corner was my father. "What are you doing here?" I asked in astonishment. He replied as if it should be obvious—"I'm always here; where did you think I would be?" I suppose after 61 years of marriage, if his spirit would linger anywhere, it would be with my mother in the house they shared for the majority of those years. Both of my dreams brought me comfort, but the truth is I wasn't sure if spirits lingered, or my dream was just a creation of my mind seeking to come to peace with the harshness of loss.

Let me get back to Bob's story because you haven't heard the best part yet. Bob's dead father-in-law not only told him everything was ok, he also gave him a cryptic message that demanded some investigation in the real living world. Bob woke thinking, as I did, that it was nice to receive comforting words from the departed, but his wife was not satisfied to leave it there. Bob had been told that the fact that everything was going well with George would be verified when he found "Wren." What or where or who could that be? How would they find out? Would their search end in nothing or was there something to this message?

Well as divine providence would have it, some time later Bob and his wife were at their son's school for a meeting, and when passing through the computer room they saw the word "Wren" in large type on a computer screen. Quickly Bob noted the web address and when he and his wife got home they looked it up. It turned out it was a female person. Now what? It didn't prove anything.

"You have to e-mail her," Bob's wife insisted.

"You must be kidding," Bob responded; "it was a dream, I'm not going to e-mail a perfect stranger about my night time reveries. She'll think I'm nuts!" Bob's wife worked on him a while and finally, with paragraphs of apologies, Bob composed an e-mail that begged the recipient not to think he had lost his marbles. He waited, anguishing, for her reply, his imagination conjuring up all manner of possible responses.

He didn't have to wait long. The next day an e-mail came

back in a tone of relief and understanding. Miss Wren replied that she had received his message with astonished delight as now she knew to whom to give the messages. She too was having dreams of her own deceased father. He told her that he had run into an old military friend named George and they were having a great old time. He asked her please to tell this man's family that he is very happy. Naturally till now she had not known to whom the message was to be delivered. She was grateful Bob had the courage to contact her.

You can imagine the effect on Bob, and especially his wife. This verification from a complete stranger of George's message made it all real. This was how Bob got started as a medium, and today he sees clients on a regular basis. He told me that when he has a session with someone for whom he has a message, he makes sure they know it is their own openness that allows that message to come across. He also encourages people to communicate with their deceased loved ones themselves.

When Bob told me his story I was very excited, recalling my own dreams. It meant they were real; my friend did visit me in my bedroom the night after he died, and my father is still close to mother and he has talked to me in my dreams. I always liked to believe this was so before, but now any doubts I had were gone.

On a recent visit to Santa Cruz I got a chance to use the gift that Bob had given me. I took a ride on a hundred-year-old steam train into the sequoia forest. The train was young in comparison to the majestic redwoods, some of which are close to three thousand years old. This hour and a half trip was the highlight of my week. The steam plumed upward, making visible the fanning shafts of sunlight streaming through the canopy above, as the bells and the urgent wailing of the steam whistle filled the air. The sounds, sights and smells filled my senses to the point I was almost in tears of sheer delight. So many times in my nearly twenty years away from home I have wished my dad could have visited me in the U.S. He would have loved to have seen this place. Right then I thought of what Bob had said about opening communication. I decided to call to my Dad from the love in my heart for him, saying please come and share this train ride with me. I waited, keeping him in my thoughts for several seconds. I thanked him for sharing the pleasure of this exciting experience and then my thoughts drifted to other things.

The Sunday after I returned from my trip, as always at church service, I closed my eyes during the Lord's Prayer to visit in my mind my family back home. There were the rows of wooden pews, the tall stained-glass depiction of the annunciation under which my family sits. There were my mother and brother and finally there was Dad. With a characteristic shoulder shrug he gave me a conspiratorial grin, as if to say, "That was fun." A wave of pleasure went through me. We shared a secret! We can now communicate because I know it's all real. If anyone saw me at church that day, I'm sure they would have wondered what I was thinking during the Lord's Prayer with my eyes closed and a broad smirk on my face. If they had cared to ask I would have replied, "Let me tell you a story, because I have a gift for you."

Love Never Dies

By S. Kay

Several years ago I had a young son about whom I was very worried. He had been mixed up in some illegal dealings and had been shot six times (three times point blank and three times in the back as he fled the shooter.) Miraculously he not only lived, but was not seriously or permanently injured. Doctors said they had never seen someone shot that many times, so close to so many major arteries and his eye, with no permanent injuries.

However he continued on the same path and I was constantly going between prayer and worry about him. One night in a dream, his father, who had died a few years before, came to me and said, "I know how worried you are about him, so I want you to know I am watching over him and you are not alone with this. I know you think this is a dream, so to prove that it is real I am going to push on your back and wake you up." I felt a strong shove on my back and woke. It was very real.

About a year after his last bout with the law, my son was coming out of a liquor store and an elderly Indian gentleman approached him and said, "Don't worry, he forgives you." My son said, "What?" and the Indian said, "Your father said he forgives you." My son and his father had not been on good terms when he died.

My husband had a very peculiar odor the last few years of his life, which was a mixture of the medications he was taking and his cologne. Very frequently, I will smell this odor; it is very distinct. I never shared this with my kids. A few months ago my daughter-in-law and I were talking about after-life possibilities, etc., and she told me that my other son was staying with them and asked her if they were using some new kind of cologne; she said no. He told her that he smelled this strange cologne which was just the way his father smelled.

My husband was a very devoted, loving father. I don't believe any man ever loved his children more. I believe his love has never died.

Living with Ghosts

By Gertrude Anne Doyle

Once I moved into this old house I was certain that there was at least one ghostly habitué. It didn't bother me as their quiet presence can be a comfort. The only bothersome thing about living with ghosts is that they sometimes move things about or open windows when it's cold outside which has happened a couple of times. Otherwise it isn't a problem; at least they don't speak out of turn, or speak at all for that matter.

The granite walls of the house are three feet thick. My dark hallway has a stairs which leads to two bedrooms and a bathroom and divides the ground floor into two equal size rooms; the room on the right is the sitting room, probably a 'parlour' in the old days and on the left a kitchen dining room. Both rooms span the depth of the house which faces the setting sun.

She appeared mostly in the sitting room, where she sat in the window seat looking out towards the front garden and gate. She appeared to be waiting. When sitting at my desk at the other side of the room, I'd see her at the corner of my eye. I often forgot about her for days, but if I'd placed a pile of books or magazines on the window seat I'd always clear them away soon after so as not to deprive her of her seat.

I met her on the stairs a few times and felt like speaking to her as she drifted past, her feet moved silently. Her movements were smooth and swift. I never met her on her way up, it was as if she only moved down stairs when I was ascending, perhaps to avoid being in the same space with me.

I once saw her in my bedroom; she was again gazing out the front window which also has a view of the gate. She had a definite form and clothes but she faded away when I looked directly at her so it was impossible to study her for more than half a second. I thought of her as 'my shape shifting woman.' I sometimes doubted the evidence of my own eyes when she disappeared like that.

The other ghost is less evident – I have felt him brush past me in the other bedroom in the left side of the house. I know it is a man because of the faint odor of pipe tobacco which lingers after him. He too favors the sitting room, and sometimes sits to the right of the fireplace on an old wooden chair. I have also seen him walk past the front gate of the house, dressed in workman's clothes from another era with a broad leather belt and braces holding up his pants. He has grey hair and a tweed cap and wears a striped collarless shirt. He too disappears when I look directly at him; I might see him at the corner of my eye and then he's gone.

The woman wore a summer dress with a floral pattern - perhaps roses; it had a flowing skirt and short cap sleeves. The colors of the dress were faded, she appeared like an old touched up black and white photo. Her features were blurred. I could not describe them because as soon as I looked directly at her she became invisible. Most of the time I forgot all about my companion; or companions I should say as the man rarely appeared.

My dog sleeps before the fire in the sitting room and does a slow reconnoiter of the room at night. He walks around and then he sniffs his bedding and paws it for a few moments before settling down. Once he stopped at the window seat and I saw his hackles rising, he sniffed and backed away. He came to rub his face against my thigh, a signal for me to pet him and fondle his neck. I never saw any other sign that he was aware of my ghostly visitors.

I became so used to my shape shifting woman that I sometimes spoke to her. "Where the hell did I leave my car keys?" I muttered to her once in a moment of frustration but then laughed at myself.

I had been living in the house for six years and had become

accustomed to her presence. I never mentioned her to anyone visiting the house. I chose not to worry people, not everyone is tolerant of otherworldly apparitions. Nobody ever mentioned my ghost.

It was in July of 2005 when I answered a knock on the door to a woman with an American accent. She was middle aged, had thick curly hair and a rosy complexion and had I seen her in the street, would have assumed she was Irish. She told me that her name was Kathleen and that her mother had died in the house about nine years before, which would have been three years before I moved in. She asked if she could come in and speak to me. She said her husband was waiting with a driver outside and so she could only stay a short while – I could see two men standing in the sunshine leaning against the taxi, smoking cigarettes.

I brought Kathleen in and she told me her story. Her mother Maud had lived here in this house with her sister Peggy and their elderly mother. Maud, at the age of 30, had conceived Kathleen out of wedlock. Kathleen knew nothing else except that soon after her birth in 1957, Maud had given her up for adoption. An American couple had taken her to New York where she had lived ever since. Just before she passed away in 2004 her adopted mother had told her of her origins and had given her the address of this house. Kathleen wept quietly as she spoke of her birth mother and the pain she must have suffered when she'd had to give up her baby. She asked if she could take some photos of the inside of the house and I took her through the rooms.

As we walked up the stairs I recalled the original smell of the musty house, the Sacred Heart picture which hung on the kitchen wall and the moth eaten clothes I had found in the bedroom cupboard when I moved in. I had cleared almost everything but held on to a few memory cards, a dog eared prayer book and a pair of gold rimmed spectacles which I'd kept in an old tea caddy ever since.

Kathleen wrote down her address in New York and asked me to contact her if I ever discovered anything about her mother and who her father had been. I promised I would make inquiries for her and write if I found out anything of interest. I gave her the tea caddy.

I did find out for Kathleen that Maud had never wed; her sister Peggy had moved away after getting married. Maud had lived out her life alone after her mother had passed away. A neighbor showed me a photograph of her taken in the 1950's, smiling for the camera. It was her sister's wedding photograph and Maud was bridesmaid. It was a summer wedding, she was dressed in an ankle length rose printed dress with cap sleeves and a small white hat with net falling over her forehead. I felt a chill as I recognized my companion of many years.

Maud had appeared to me as she had been in her prime and had remained in the house waiting at the front window.

After the visit of her daughter, I never saw Maud's apparition again. But the gray haired man still lingers and sometimes sits by my fireside.

When Dreams Come True

By Dearbhla Egan

The first encounter I had around a dream "coming true" happened many years ago, and the dream was not mine, it was my mother's. When I was in my late teens my mother told me about a dream she had had shortly after she got married. My mother was quite a conservative and private person when it came to discussing matters of sex and sexuality as were most people in Ireland at that time, so her dream came as something of a surprise. She told me that in the dream she had spent a rather "naughty" night with the local jeweler. As she was planning to visit his shop the next day to leave in a watch to be repaired, she supposed he was on her mind and that was the reason for the dream. However, when my mother entered the shop the next day, the jeweler, who shall remain nameless, sidled up to her at the counter and whispered, "Wow, Fran, I had a great time with you last night," and he winked. My mother was mortified and got out of the shop as quickly as she could. She told me all of this in a kind of conspiratorial whisper. Of course she never told my father about the dream, but she was perplexed for the rest of her life that both she and the jeweler had shared an intimate experience together through a dream they had had on the same night. It could hardly be described as a deep and meaningful spiritual meeting of souls, but it was never just a coincidence either. I can only say for sure that it was the absolute truth, as I know for sure my mother would not have told me about it otherwise.

The first really lucid dreams I began to experience and remember clearly in wakefulness began to happen during my early twenties. In these dreams I was flying. It was as though I was a huge bird swooping and soaring over my home and the hinterlands around it. I could clearly feel the wind coursing across my face and body and a feeling of real exhilaration as I swooped and dived over the houses and fields of my neighbors' farms and houses. I always had a strong feeling that I was not "flying solo" on these occasions—that there was another flyer or presence there with me, watching me and keeping me safe. On waking from these dreams I felt certain that I had indeed been airborne during sleep. How else could I have seen what I saw from that elevated perspective? I had been flying, for sure, but of course I kept my aeronautical experiences to myself. With my record, it didn't take a lot for people to conclude that I was nuts! I had this dream repeatedly every few weeks for about ten years, and then it stopped and I have not flown by myself since then.

In my early thirties, my mother, with whom I was very close, was diagnosed with cancer of the thyroid gland. Within three months she was dead. I immediately began to fall into a downward spiral emotionally. I was in the early stages of a complete breakdown and felt terribly vulnerable, lost and bereft. I could not conceive of a life without her. She was my all. I started to lose weight at an alarming rate. My hair began to fall out through stress and lack of nutrition. I was unable to sleep, and wakefulness was a nightmare of the most awful proportions. One afternoon, in desperation, I took a sleeping pill and went to bed. I fell into a deep, exhausted sleep during which I had one of the most memorable dreams of my life. It was a short and simple dream but meant everything to me.

I dreamt that I was standing in the kitchen of the home where I grew up. There was an archway in the wall that separated the kitchen from the dining room. I was standing under this archway between the two rooms when I became aware that my mother was standing facing me. She did not say anything but smiled at me and reached out to embrace me. She was wearing a red wool sweater that she favored before she died, and as she held me, I could feel the texture of the sweater and the warmth

142

of her body through my hands. She held me close to her for just a few moments and I remember feeling unwilling to let her go. She moved away from me gently, and just as quickly as she had appeared, she was gone. I awoke from my sleep with tears coursing down my face, but feeling a sense of peace that I had begun to believe I would never feel again. My mother came to me that day because her child was in deep trouble, and just as she would have comforted me in life, she comforted me in death.

During the course of my life I had always had a very troubled relationship with my father. Through personal experience, I now believe that he may have suffered from Bipolar Disorder like me, but I did not understand that as a child or young adult, and saw his erratic behavior as a rejection of me and an inability to love his own children. Oh how I longed for him to change and let me know in some way that he cared, that he loved, but of course it never happened; and then, three years ago he died. I felt nothing—or so I thought. Because I did not cry or feel regretful or bereft, I believed that I had finally come to terms with who my father was, with all his faults and failings. Then, just a few weeks ago, again during an afternoon nap, I had two very lucid dreams.

In the first dream I was sitting up in bed when a soft knock came at the door and my mother entered my room. She was a younger woman, dressed in a yellow sundress. She came to my side, sat on the bed and said, "This will have to be quick because I'm in a hurry, but I just need to tell you that I love you;" and she laughed, her lovely raucous laugh, as she hugged me before she left the room.

The dream ended there, but then another knock came on the door of my room where I was again sitting up in bed. This time my father entered, looking much as he did before he died. He too came to my bedside and sat down, embraced me and said, "You know I always loved you, Derv?" and I started to cry. My dad gently brushed the tears from my face and then he left the room. I woke up at this point feeling very upset, but again, certain beyond doubt that my parents had come to see me. I have lately been giving much thought to the words my father spoke and am beginning to believe that they might very well be true. Imagine the sense of peace that allowing myself to believe this brings. I have also learned from my heartfelt reaction to him in the dream that I did and still do love my father. What an amazing gift to think that there was still time for us to reconcile after he died.

The Watchers

By Chrystine Julian

A spiritual teacher for which I am thankful is the Kern River. It is a significant contributor to my learning and personal transformation. We became good friends as over a period of years I made regular visits to observe it in a variety of moods, from day and night, summer and winter, sun and storm.

During those sessions, while sitting along the banks I learned songs; in the middle of the flow I discovered a voice that drowned reality. I sensed the rush of earth's life blood as it fell from the mountains. I felt the loneliness as it empties into a field, being a river without a sea. Its purpose is not joining a pool; this river exists only to flow. Known as the Killer Kern, it is a schoolmaster, it brings life in addition to carrying death.

On one of my visits I came to understand the existence of the ones I call The Watchers, part of the earth both indigenous and ancient. It is not uncommon in mythic and mystical traditions for beings to assume other forms or reveal themselves through inanimate objects.

Up the canyon from Bakersfield towards Lake Isabella, at a spot near the edge of the river I found a flat boulder with indentations similar to ones I have seen in archeological sites that had been used by indigenous for grinding grain and nuts. That led me to suspect that this might have at some distant time in the past been a tribal home site.

I sat and observed in silence. I noticed the plants, birds, variety of rocks and the flow patterns of the river. Then something unusual caught my eye; human and animal stone images were clearly distinguishable among the rocks and cliff along the far side of the river. There was a queen, complete with ceremonial headdress, surrounded by several members of her court. Above them at the top of the ridge was an outcropping in the image of a mammoth. The tribe seemed fixated in an eastward gaze; but with unhappy facial expressions.

Using the roar of the river as my drumbeat, I did a shamanic journey in an attempt to connect with these beings.

What transpired cannot be called a conversation in English, but rather a collection of impressions and sensations. I emerged from the meditative state with the understanding that a group of people had opted to become part of the earth rather than pass on into the spirit world. Based on the image of the mammoth, I placed them in a pre-ice age period. Whatever they were waiting for had not transpired, and they seemed tired of their current state.

One of the shamanic skills I discovered early on in my training is the ability to assist people with cutting ties to this world and moving on. So I did another brief journey on behalf of the watchers to assist them in finding freedom.

A few weeks later a friend and I were taking a trip up through the canyon and stopped at the spot. I tried to point out the images in the rocks, but they were gone.

There are several possible explanations: perhaps the images were the result of shadows cast under peculiar conditions that are not constant, the spirits in the rocks were not comfortable revealing their presence to another person, or maybe they changed their minds and moved on to the next realm.

I have no vested interest in any of the potential conclusions, but share the story here only as an example of alternative ways to connect with the world.

I Knew That's Why
I Felt Love in My Heart!

By Christy Shelton

My grandmother Sophie used to cheer for me from the front porch as I would leave for work or school in the mornings. Imagine how that feels to be so loved and supported! This heartfelt generosity of Spirit was emblematic of who Sophie was—a deeply kind, innocently beautiful, devout Catholic woman who loved unconditionally. Although her physical body has long since de-materialized from this Earth plane, her Spirit continues to have a presence in my life through a love bond that was set in motion between us long ago—or perhaps it always was, and as this story will reveal—always will be.

To set the stage, here is a little background about my maternal grandmother, whom I call "Nana." Being the youngest of *eleven* children from a Lithuanian family, my grandmother stayed at home longer than most of her generation to take care of her ailing mother until she passed. Then in her late 20's, Nana met and married a Russian musician after only having exchanged *letters* with him; together they immigrated to New York and had two daughters who were thirteen years apart. I never met my grandfather because he was "not a good man." The full gravity of his abusive behavior was made known by my mother as she prepared for her wedding—upon hearing about this, the priest said to my grandmother, "God never intended you to suffer in marriage! Leave him with my blessings." Released from her Catholic vow of "till death do us part," Nana divorced him, moved to California, and supported herself and her youngest daughter by working as a seamstress. Although she never got a driver's license, she was independent, and managed to save

147

enough to buy a Spanish-style house that had four apartment units behind it and a large rose garden.

I loved staying over night at Nana's house, listening to her say the rosary; seeing the violets blooming on every windowsill; watching her wash her nylons in the bathroom sink and carefully hang them up to dry on the shower rod; exploring the storerooms with endlessly fascinating objects from another era; playing on the dark, shiny upright piano, and feeding her cross-eyed Siamese cat, "Sloopy." Nana took me to church with her on Sundays, where I developed a lifelong connection with Jesus and Mary. She taught me how to pray "Now I lay me down to sleep" and the Lord's Prayer, but also that prayer could be *anything spoken from your heart to God.* She gave the example of how she prayed as a child by hopping from stone to stone across a river saying— *"this step is for you, God, this step is for me; this step is for you, God, this step is for me."*

We all enjoyed having Sunday dinners there—my Mom, Dad, two brothers and I—usually a hardy brisket with carrots and potatoes. The meal would begin with one of us saying grace, and invariably end with her saying, "and God Bless America!" She made magnificent Slavic desserts like "Rabbit Ears"—a thin pastry, delicately cut and folded to look like a rabbit's ear, then deep fried and sprinkled with powdered sugar—or the "Zabaglione Cake"—a recipe given to her by a former Italian neighbor in Brooklyn that was a light meringue cake covered with fresh whipped cream, cut strawberries and rum sauce on the side! Whether we were at her house or she was at ours, Nana always had hard candy in her purse for my brothers and me, and would regularly squeeze folded up dollar bills into the palms of our hands saying, "You take it honey, you take it."

Nana came to live with us after she started developing Alzheimer's, when I was in my late teens and into my early twenties. As the disease progressed, she forgot our names but not her love for us. Once when I was visiting her after I'd moved out, she did not remember my name. "Nana," I said, "it's me

Christy, your granddaughter." A smile spread across her face and tears welled up in her eyes—"*Oh, Christinka, I knew that's why I felt love in my heart!*"

There were countless ways in which my grandmother showed up in her life, and in mine, as pure love, but none so eternally giving as what she showed me three weeks *after* she made her transition. I was missing her terribly, and deeply longing to feel a connection with her—and at the same time, wanted her approval of a romantic relationship I was in. Early one morning about three or four a.m., I was awakened by a voice of what I have come to believe was an ancestor, as it spoke with a Lithuanian accent, and because Nana was from such a large, close-knit family. The female voice said "*Christinka, we have a message for you from your grandmother—she wants you to know that she loves you very much and just wants you to be happy.*" Then I felt my entire body being "x-rayed," "scanned," "flooded" with radiant white light—the experience was that I was *completely seen*—every square inch and molecule, and that despite my own withholding and self judgments, there was in actuality no part of me that was unlovable. I felt totally loved and accepted. Next, my grandmother appeared before me, and unzipped her old body from the top of her head down, parting the skin as if it were a garment, to reveal her new or true self inside—a beautiful young woman.

I am infinitely grateful to my grandmother for this direct experience with pure unconditional love, which has become a touchstone for building and grounding my faith throughout my life. As a result, I do not believe in death anymore but in one Life—because I ultimately know that eternal love is all there is … I love you Nana!

Writing

The little time spent in the quiet each day, alone with one's God, that we may make and keep our connection with the Infinite source—our source and our life—will be a boon to any life. It will prove, if we are faithful, to be the most priceless possession that we have.
- Emerson

Writing is a wonderful therapy. Sitting down in quiet, freely writing out our concerns, our deepest fears, our confused emotions, our doubts, even our worst-case scenarios has the benefit of freeing our minds to be present in the moment. It is as if when we lay out the darkest thoughts, hidden till then in the recesses of our minds, we are allowing light to be shed on them, dispelling their ominous shadow on our lives.

Reading the written word of inspirational authors is a wonderful way to help us direct and clarify our own thoughts. Classic novels are allegories of life's vicissitudes, the comedy and the tragedy that make up all human experiences. In them we may gain perspective on our own lives as we see our own darkness and light reflected there.

If you are working out a problem, I invite you to pick up a pen and write. If you have a question use your imagination to write what Universal Wisdom might say in answer. You will be surprised how wise you are. If you make a habit of writing, over time you will see greater clarity come into your thinking.

If writing is not your medium, talk with a Spiritual counselor or trusted friend. Ask them to simply listen. Tell your story in third person and see how it feels. As you hear your own words spoken, it is as if you gain the perspective of an observer, which allows new insights.

Going Forward

By Joan Doyle

It was June, and as I moved around my home doing laundry, I sang an Irish song to myself. Musing on my recent trip to Ireland celebrating my engagement to Justin, I was recalling how Justin had loved Ireland and my family had loved him. We had set the date for our wedding, and although we still lived in our separate homes we had made our first major purchase together. We had bought a washer/dryer. My ten-year-old washer finally gave up the ghost despite Justin's valiant efforts to resuscitate it. All things were moving forward and I had a deep sense that this relationship was a true gift from Spirit, which is not to say we did not come across the occasional bump in the road or fear to be faced. I felt I had found a safe place. I could be my imperfect and vulnerable self as well as my strong and competent self and be loved whatever way I showed up. I was very happy.

At times I wondered where this great guy had come from and how I had gotten so lucky. Whenever I had these thoughts, rather than disbelieve how good things could be or wonder if I was worthy of this love, I would simply say, "Thank you God, thank you Spirit." It was my way of accepting the gift, allowing myself to be loved. Otherwise, my old deprecating thoughts might convince me I did not deserve him, and I didn't want to sabotage something so good.

Early on, when I recognized I was interested in Justin romantically but we had not yet started dating, I remember a day when I found myself thinking about him almost obsessively. When would he call? Did he feel the same as I was beginning to feel? There was an anxiety that felt unhealthy and uncomfortable. Journaling helps a lot when I feel the need to process things; it gets things out of my head so I can think more clearly. I took a moment to write.

In writing I knew that the longing we feel for another is really about wanting connection. This connection is to ourselves, firstly, to others secondly, and to all life, ultimately. While writing I realized that I simply admired this man and he was in my life one way or another, as friend or acquaintance. I knew I could not control how he felt, only how I responded to how I felt. The process of giving space to my rational and irrational mind in writing helped me center myself. I was able to release any need I had for him to show up any way other than as he was, a delightful soul on his path, showing me an example of someone who lived authentically and in integrity with his beliefs.

As a result of the clarity I received in writing, I decided I would call him rather than wait in hope that he would call me. He was not home. I left a message to say just how much I appreciated how he lived and who he was and how glad I was to know him. It felt so good to acknowledge another. In that moment, I felt connected with myself and the love that I could give. It was a very empowering experience. I felt love by giving love. I think I fell in love then, with the life in me, with the possibilities that this knowledge of my ability to create love showed me.

Love and joy do not arrive when we meet our soul mate. How much pleasure and life would we deprive ourselves of in the mean time? I knew then that I could still have a wonderful, love-filled and delightful life even if I never met my perfect mate. Of course you know that's not how the story ends.

On that June evening more than a year after that phone call, I was pulling clothes out of the dryer we had bought together when I heard Justin call to me from my open front door. At that same moment, a shiny Wisconsin quarter bounced out of the sheet I was pulling on and landed at my feet. I picked it up and read the word on its face: it said in capital letters, FORWARD. Yes, we were moving forward, beautifully and happily. Keeping in mind that wonderful lesson of my own power to create love as I looked at the coin, I just said a silent prayer, "Thank you God."

My Love Affair with Truth and Fiction

By Sabrina Johnson

A friend of mine reminds me of what I used to say when she'd ask me if I'd read some bestselling self-help book. She tells me that I'd declare: "I don't need self-help books. I have my classics." This has been true for most of my adult life, except that now I must make a disclaimer before I continue. In the past few years, I have read one or two self-help books. This is because I no longer shun any books that come across my path.

I'm more open to reading various genres of books, including self-help, because I'm a writer who enjoys living and writing about inner transformation. I call it...*the journey back home from whence I first came, before I was born of flesh and bone.*

It's the journey of knowing who I am beyond my body, my thoughts, words, and actions—beyond anything I can humanly define; and yet it's what I humanly experience, with an awareness that is heightened by a deeper understanding. This deeper understanding is attained through many means: prayer, mediation and contemplation, as well as reading metaphysical and secular literature—knowing that the division between the two is only a matter of perception.

The perception with which I read secular books is the same way I perceive the world about me, which is seeing beyond the physical, changing conditions to the unchanging Spiritual Truth. Of course, I'm human and sometimes fall into the seduction of believing what I see and hear, trusting my five senses more than the Infinite Wisdom of Spirit.

This occurs more so when it comes to some belief I've acquired about myself that is not true, no longer serves me, and yet, like an old blanket that is worn thin and torn, feels like it still provides some comfort and protection. But it doesn't provide anything except a shoddy covering over the Truth of who I am.

Vipassana meditation, also known as mindfulness or insight meditation is an important part of this seeing rightly. When it was first suggested to me, I readily began to study and practice this inner art. I was morbidly obese and in the midst of a four-year accreditation program to become a spiritual counselor. There was a part of me that knew in order to be a conduit through which Spirit could work, I needed to be clear. Stuffing myself with food, and as a result burdening my body temple with excess layers of fat, was not conducive to such clarity.

But the clarity came, as did the resulting freedom from compulsive overeating and the restoration of my body temple to a moderate weight. Through meditation I've learned to be a compassionate witness of myself and others.

One thing I witnessed in myself was an old belief of "not belonging." I believed I just didn't fit in, wherever I was. This was no longer a matter of physically fitting in because I was no longer obese. It was a feeling of being separate and apart from others, and separate and apart from the God within me, as me.

As a child, I learned that reading was a way in which I could fit in, easily and effortlessly. I became kindred spirits with Anne of Green Gables. Nancy Drew never excluded me from joining her and her girlfriends in driving around town in her father's big shiny car. And she never made fun of me if I was too scared to join her on her stealth missions to uncover some mystery.

Later on, as an unhappy young adult, this ability to move into a story and become part of it helped me feel less alienated when I read works such as Dostoevsky's *Notes from the Underground*. The "Underground Man" was truly miserable, and at times I felt that way, too, and so I knew I wasn't alone in my misery. Being able to immerse and plunge myself into a story allowed me to have my need to feel connected and to belong met by the level of engagement I felt. I still read with this active imagination. Today, however, I engage in my secular reading just as I do with all of life, with that heart of my compassionate witness, with whom I have become familiar in meditation.

One morning while meditating, I found myself being drawn over again to thinking about one particular passage in Barbara Kingsolver's *The Poisonwood Bible*, which I'd just read. It was about Adah, the physically and mentally slow, awkward, ugly duckling twin of beautiful butterfly-like Leah. Adah describes how she and her siblings would travel through the outskirts of the remote African village where their missionary father brought them to live—Leah first, the others following, and Adah last. Adah calls herself "the monster, Quasimodo," limping as she uses her left side to drag her right side behind her. This results in a "stepsong sing" with a chorus of *"left...behind, left...behind."* I too limped, pulling one leg forward while dragging the next one to meet it. I also felt like a monster with this shuffle and drag walk. I also felt left behind. Adah's story is that when she becomes an adult, she learns she is not mentally slow, but a genius. She becomes an esteemed doctor of the sciences and learns how to retrain herself so that she can walk without a limp. She's no longer left behind.

As I thought of Adah while mediating, I realized that Spirit was talking to me, telling me that I, like Adah, no longer needed to believe that I was a monster, or that I was left behind. I too was a genius, and through the Infinite Intelligence of God I was learning how to self-heal and walk without a limp in my physical body or mental thoughts. For me this is one of the most enjoyable ways I listen to Spirit talk to me—through stories, whether it's classics or modern fiction.

Hindsight

By Mary Hylan

One morning recently I was looking for a certain old journal after a colleague/friend's passing; I pull it out annually to write about the past year and sometimes to record important life events.

Jumping out at me as I opened the found journal was a letter stuck in the back—a yellow, legal pad note. I knew what it was immediately, and the memory was not a pleasant one. It was a handwritten letter from twenty five years ago—my sister-in-law expounding on a disagreement we had had which resulted in a major rift in the family. I had sometimes had difficulty relating with her, and apparently the reverse was also true.

After this, I was not allowed to see the children. This was absolutely devastating, one of the most painful things of my life—cut off from my adorable little ones that I loved so much— no matter what they thought! It all felt so unjust. The punishment seemed so much worse to me than the crime. "Why me?!" had been my predominant thought then. I hadn't done anything *that* bad! I had only the best of intentions. I was the middle-child, peacemaker who wanted everyone to be happy and harmonious, the loving, caring one in a sometimes critical family atmosphere.

I remember responding to this letter saying I could un- derstand how she could perceive that I hadn't been totally thoughtful and considerate, that maybe I was too desirous of my own way. And it was true that I did not understand parent-child relationships so well: I was not a parent. I tried to make peace. This was still unacceptable to her. My brother had sided with her, as often happens, and responded once to a remark about my having good intentions with the phrase about the road to hell being paved with good intentions; ouch. Over the years, however, I had worked on forgiveness for her, some for my brother and me, and did redevelop a nice relationship with him, and a mellowing of it all.

In this moment, with the letter before me, I have no wish to revisit this painful situation, but some unknown, inner courage impels me to open the brilliant yellow pages and hear the words again from some twenty five years before. Why did this, this yellow paper, come up to the surface again? It must be time to totally forgive her.

As I read I am stunned by how completely different the letter is to what I remember: the language is not ranting, rigid, nasty, hateful. She sounds, mostly... absolutely reasonable! Not scathing, but clear and direct. What...?!! I'm stunned, stricken.

I see her point of view. I could see me doing that. I feel the disrespect I had displayed sometimes for their parenting and relationship—trying to impose my ways, questioning them, speaking out of turn, judging. I felt self-condemned, for a minute. Oh my god, I did this? And this? No, it didn't feel totally unfamiliar. And then...worse—that could be me now, STILL! I could still see myself doing some of those things even now, in different situations.

I felt compassion for her in that moment, and regret for my ignorance and arrogance. I could still feel a spark of victimization, but reading her words again, I knew that because of all of the spiritual work I'd done in the interim, victimhood was not an option. Yes, I did these things, even if perhaps less than she perceived and more than I had thought.

A truer acceptance of my part was dawning on me. I had to move forward—first, in forgiving *myself*. I had to realize that I can be obnoxious even now! We all can. I believe that there is no human perfection, but there *is* Spiritual Perfection—something good in each of us that is beyond tainting.

The yellow paper had done its work. It was a sign that it was time—time to remind myself how far I've come, recognizing that each day reveals still more work to be done. The letter compelled me to continue exploring and to write this story, another major healing step.

It comes down to a few life lessons: I can have the courage to admit that I am human, perfectly imperfect, and still worthy and lovable. I am a child of God, loved, no matter what. I now see more clearly that this relates to others, and feel the freedom that comes from experiencing compassion and forgiveness for them, in *their* humanness.

So although I am on a committed spiritual path and feel I'm growing in understanding and wisdom, I still have a ways to go to soften my edges and judge not, to allow others their own path, and turn my attention to my own work. I am willing. As in the 50's TV show when Lucy was told she'd "got some splainin' to do!" Spirit is saying to me, "Mary...you got some growin' to do!" And that's ok.

The Ring - Circle of Love

By Joan Doyle

In my mind's eye I can see the ring on my mother's ninety-year-old finger. It sits next to her wedding and engagement rings that she complains keep slipping around, and which she was hoping to corral with this new addition. It hasn't worked; nevertheless, she likes the ring. It is a broad silver ring, open and adjustable, which is a good thing, as I needed to open it to get it over her knuckle and tighten it again on the thinner part of her finger. Her knuckles are enlarged with the arthritis that has ravaged her body and keeps her now wheelchair-bound. The ring has a raised, detailed design in Sanskrit. It doesn't mean anything to her, this writing that she cannot identify; she likes its appearance. It's her daughter's ring, my ring.

She was admiring the rings on my fingers. I was wearing five rings at the time and she asked if they were new. "No," I said, "I have a little drawer full of rings and I interchange them." "Give me one," she said, her dark eyes twinkling in contrast to her silver hair. She has never worn another ring but her wedding rings—no time for such goster, and more to the point, no money. It was far from Sanskrit or silver, she was reared. She's a woman, maybe an old woman, but like the rest of us women she likes shiny things.

I have to say I was taken aback by her direct request. I hesitated, but only for a moment. I would give her the shirt off my back if she asked for it. She never asks for anything. A light spirit, she feels she has all she needs. She wants for nothing. "Don't buy me anything for Christmas," she says every year. "I have enough."

All her life she has given away good things. If we got a gift of a new set of dinnerware, she'd be plotting who she could give it to: who was getting married or setting up home? We continued to use a perfectly serviceable, mix-and-match set with more than its fair share of chips and cracks. "We can't take it with us when we go," she'd say; "let it go to someone who needs it more than we do." With a house-full of children she still found something to give to a traveler or neighbor in need. Her generosity was an expression of her gratitude for her own blessings. By today's standards it might be said that she had few. Having been orphaned at the age of five and taken in by a spinster aunt, she knew loss and hardship none of her children would ever know.

Smart and intelligent, she chose her life partner well, and together they created a life that was luxurious for their children, in comparison with their own early years. Running water, electric lights, television, good schools and they scrimped to send us to college. We were the first generation in either family line to enjoy that privilege.

It's human nature to look at what we don't have rather than what we do, but in her case I witnessed an exception when it came to material things. As a child I did not appreciate their achievements. I saw friends with new clothes—not hand-me-downs, ABBA albums, pocket money, and I wanted them but could not have them. I stole pennies at age seven. I cried if I could not go on a school outing. I begged and pleaded for patent leather shoes and when I got them, decided they were just not the right style. I tested my parents' patience and stretched their pocket book. My brother remembers being very aware of the financial stresses underlying our family life. I detested how my mother in her wisdom would say, "Want will be your master." With maturity I look back with a new perspective. I am almost ashamed of my childish wanting; except that I know it is our human nature.

I think of my ring on her finger; it was an early engagement ring—a promise to marry my husband after we had only been dating six months. It came wrapped elaborately and with much thought and though I accepted it, for I knew it was right, I asked that we keep it a secret for a while. It just seemed such a whirlwind. I wondered what my sensible parents and friends would say about our impetuousness.

I wore the ring with its Sanskrit, six-syllable message, Om Mani Padme Hum, for several months. The meanings of the symbols cannot be directly translated but they embody the idea of enlightened awareness. It is a mantra believed by Buddhists to contain the entire truth about the nature of suffering and the many ways of removing its causes. When Justin and I made our engagement official, it was replaced with a diamond and emerald family heirloom.

The simple silver ring is imbued with our new love, with passion and impetuousness and deep knowing of the rightness of things. It is a part of my history and now it sits next to my mother's wedding rings, precious symbols of the love of a good man and a wise woman. The thought makes me very happy. Besides, we can't take it with us. When we give a gift, it is a piece of our heart left with another and the more precious the object, the deeper the joy in giving.

Post Script; Though we talk weekly, my mother and I both love the exchange of writing through the mail with letters and clippings of poetry or articles of interest. I let my mother read this story, thus far, sometime last year. This year, for my fiftieth birthday, she sent me something that has been very precious to her. It is a large, sterling silver "Child of Mary" medal inscribed with her maiden name and the date June 2nd 1935. Young women in the society of the "Children of Mary" were given such a medal only after they had requested to join, and then for six months lived according to their virtues of sacrifice, prayer, and works of charity. She must have been proud at the tender age of fourteen to receive such a medal that her aunt must have splurged to purchase. She wore it on a blue ribbon, and I know, next to her wedding rings, it is her dearest material possession. My brother tried to dissuade her from sending it to me after wearing it for seventy-seven years but she was determined.

I received her message of love with floods of tears. She is leaving a piece of her heart with me and I cannot deny the bitter-sweetness of the gift. My friend Mary's words come to my mind and comfort me: "My heart is always with you and my heart is more real than my body." Neither distance nor death can separate us from those we have loved or been loved by. The love between a mother and a daughter is a sacred connection. Love transcends all and this truth soothes me, as does the wearing of my mother's medal next to my own heart.

The Pinecones

By Carrie McConkey-Herrera

On a perfect, sunny day in May, I was running up the hill, and while I am always delighted to see pinecones that have fallen to the ground, I somehow always feel surprised, as if pinecones only belong back East somewhere. I remember decorating our home with them for Christmas and using them for school art projects. You know, red and green spray paint and gold glitter.

Living in California, I feel I only see them in the stores around the holidays. They always have that stinky, fake smell of cinnamon. Anyhow, on this particular day, I was amazed at how large this particular pinecone was, and I thought, *I will grab this on the way back down the hill to bring home to my three-year-old son, Diego.*

OK…so here I am jogging with this rather large pinecone and I come across another one, and while it is not large, it is almost perfectly shaped, and *Well*, I figured, *why not? It will even me out if I carry one in each hand.*

As I bent down and picked up this perfectly shaped pinecone, I discovered it was much heavier than the very large pinecone I was already holding. So, I realized that this very large pinecone was so large and so beautiful, and that every part of it was open, and it felt light. The bottom of it reminded me, somehow, of a flower that had bloomed completely, and it felt smooth and sturdy, and even as I handle it now, it is still a little sticky and has the aroma of pine.

The smaller, perfectly shaped pinecone was so much heavier and dense. It was not open at all and felt so prickly to the touch, and there was not yet that formed flower at the bottom, but it was definitely sticky.

As I sit here writing about these two pinecones—how they

are different and their sticky similarity—I realize they are both of God. They both came from a huge, magnificent tree that was rooted in God's earth. They are made of exactly the same God stuff. The large pinecone, although there were external elements like wind, rain, and birds, held on to that tree for as long as it could to completely open up and become a large, magnificent pinecone. Its energy has been shared with me, and now you, through this story.

The heavier, denser pinecone fell away from the tree early on, never having the chance to open up, but certainly it was perfect, and now I also share that energy with you.

You see, we are all made up of God's energy. We are also all perfect and even the one's that are of the utmost perfection, there is always work to do around the sticky stuff!

The other day I went running again, as I do, and I found the cutest, tiniest pinecone I had ever seen…this one was smooth, light, had flower shapes on the bottom and top, it smelled of pine, but it didn't have one sticky thing about it…the little ones really are the truest of God's perfection.

Grand, Mother Love

By Mary Hylan

I love to read, and Spirit often speaks to me through the written word. Two powerful experiences I had lately remind me of the sweet, ancient, living love we all share.

My mother had a lot of beautiful old books from her childhood. Although I hadn't read many, I cherished them and kept them after she passed on four years ago. Her birthday date recently called me to share time with her. I picked up a classic book I'd never read, with a painted picture set on a beautiful, blue-cloth cover and gold lettering that said, *Jane Eyre*. I wanted to touch pages of something she touched, read a book she'd read, share a story...

My mother's clear, youthful inscription met me: Helen G. and the year 1928. I stopped, tingling—she was just a girl then, reading this book. And in this moment we're sharing, I am late middle-aged, and she's fifteen! Things are reversed; we are joined through the mists of time and timelessness. And moreover, at another point *she* was sixty years old and I, twenty. She's old, I'm young; I'm old, she's young—past and present mingling in the same moment. What a mind-boggling juxtaposition!

While reading, I felt, in this spacious realm, *Mom and I are reading the same book*. We both held it, turned the ragged-edged pages of the day, read the same words, the same story...beyond time and space. I thought about Jane and all of us "characters" and our similarities—fascinating! I wondered how Mom had responded to this or that. She was not so far away from that time, and now I could gratefully understand more about her and her culture. Jane's wonderings and turmoil, strength and clear-headedness—we all shared these life experiences. I came back to the eternal Now. *What does she think, feel now? "Mom, can you sense this?"* I consciously connected with all this bridging of experience and chronology throughout the book, which I was hesitant to finish and release.

Traveling back and forth through infinity captured in a moment, I would feel this sort of a glowing around me and within as I read: this warmth, love, oneness, an interconnectedness hard to express in my beloved words—*beyond* words. I delighted and thrilled in the experience of my mother and me curled up together on my comfortable couch reading the same book. A delicious little secret we shared—I, with a Mona Lisa smile on my face.

This heart-opening to great, motherly love prepared me for the second instance. It emerged through a magazine story about a woman's learnings from her grandmother. At first I had resisted reading this story as I'd felt I had never really had a grandma (and one brief, faraway grandfather,) and sometimes I'd felt I had missed something; I didn't want to be reminded. Today I was to read it and deeply take it in.

Her description of her grandmother struck me and gave me pause: Grandmother always answered, was never annoyed or hurried, and was infinitely encouraging and nurturing. I stopped for a long while to bask in imagining, to give myself the feeling of... "Grandma." I felt the warm arms, the smile, the tender voice of that ideal grandma, offering cookies and hot chocolate, listening to my tales from school. Never a harsh word spoken, never was she irritated or critical. I felt cared for as rarely before, with a childlike expectancy of good, and a profound sense of being heard, known and seen, precious, capable, and adored.

Someone was appreciating me deeply. I suddenly realized— that is my God! That is *my* idea of God. That is who always loves me as I am, completely, and is always gently answering and giving me deep, underlying security and freedom. If I listen, Spirit tells me how wonderful I am. I get it!

I momentarily reflected on "God as Grandparent," taking a

side trip to *what about fathers?* The idea and the feeling of "Grandfather" rose as protective, providing, humorous, and full of life and energy. I saw me sitting on his knee with an arm around me, or walking with my hand in his, nudging me forward, showing me the world.

I had this deep felt-sense of God, of unconditional, Mother-Father Love: a stress-less, grand-parenting kind of love. Whereas mothers may get harried and frustrated, and fathers, angry or tired—God doesn't. Spirit always has time, is present, and is Love. I heard a sweet, elderly lady say once, "I just crawl up on God's lap..." Now I understand this. I never physically had a Grandma (or "grandparent,") but I do now!

I know that we can do it. We can sit on the couch and reach and feel across space and the ages, sharing these truly heartwarming times of Grand-parenting Love; Grand, Mother Love. Call it what you will—deep, infinite, absolute Love. For anyone who loves or yearns to reconnect with feelings of beloved grandparents, of motherly-fatherly love, I invite you right now to imagine, for yourself, that warm embrace, gentle voice, and loving arms...

The List

By Julie Penman Livesey

In the sixteen years since I left college, I had lived in fourteen different abodes, in five different cities, in three different countries. Now I was going to be on the move again.

I was helping my current landlady trim and tie up her rose bushes when she announced that she was putting her house on the market and skiddaddling out of state as quickly as she could. The housing market had gone sky high and she was about to make at least 200 percent profit on her home of ten years. I had just three weeks to find somewhere else to live.

As luck would have it, a friend of mine knew of someone who was looking for a tenant for the little apartment under her house, and before I knew it, I had said "YES!" and was packing my bags.

It was the teeniest tiniest place anyone could ever imagine, but it was cheerfully decorated and separate from the rest of the house above me, giving me the privacy I had so lacked at my previous home. It sat at the top of a steep hill, allowing an expansive view of the city and mountains around me when out on the deck.

As I unpacked my belongings and tried to make my few pieces of furniture fit into three hundred or so square feet of space that was now my home, I could not help but lament the nomadic lifestyle that I had created for myself and my long suffering cat, Gavroche. When was the constant moving going to end, I asked myself, wearily. I was thirty-seven, still single and in danger of becoming one of those crazy old cat ladies. It was then and there, my path blocked in every direction by piles of boxes, that I mentally declared an intention that I WOULD NOT

MOVE AGAIN until I was moving in with Him—the sweet, chu-chi faced man out there somewhere, that I would share the rest of my life with. A few days later, when I was finally able to reach the armchair, I remembered something a friend had suggested. I sat down and wrote a list of a hundred qualities that I would like this man to have, a written affirmation that I was ready for such a man, and that I would recognize him when he entered my life. It was a pretty comprehensive list, covering everything from his build, interests and beliefs, tastes, personality and background, to how he would make me feel about myself and how wonderfully he would enhance my life through his being in it etc., etc. I even requested such details as a love of singing, that he be a great cook, and have a Scottish accent! The list completed to my satisfaction, I placed it in my sock drawer for safe keeping.

Soon after I had settled in, Sinead, my new landlady, decided to move back to Ireland, leaving the house in the care of her now deceased partner's son, Tommy. He would live in the main house upstairs, and I would give my monthly rent to him.

As the months went by, I felt very happy and at peace in my new, albeit, tiny home. I was getting plenty of animation work, either freelance or in-house and had a pretty good social life. From time to time, I would take out the list and read it over, in order to remind myself of this person I was to keep my heart open for. Then I would slip it back into the drawer and forget about it for a while.

Suddenly, it seemed, the U.S. economy went down the toilet. A huge job I was working on was immediately cancelled, meaning a good few months of promised work was now gone. A sense of dread was seizing the country. Nervous about my future, I was thankful for the wonderfully low rent and the savings I had managed to squirrel away. I was not getting as much work now and money was tight, but it was still enough for me to live relatively comfortably on. The fact that Tommy was not working and had become rather reclusive began to worry me, but whenever I managed to catch him, he insisted that all was well.

Then I got a most distressed call from Sinead. She had just learned that Tommy had not been paying the mortgage or the property tax, and had not done so for over a year. He had been paying some, but not all, of the utilities, and was feeding himself with my rent. Barring a miracle happening, the house would be forced into foreclosure. I probably had about three weeks to get out.

I looked around me and just screamed "NO, NO, NO!!" This was not meant to happen. I was not supposed to leave until I had found my chu-chi faced man! For days, I cried and I panicked and I threw things around in anger, and I gave Tommy a piece of my mind. I ate quite a lot of chocolate too—but I didn't start to pack. Something kept telling me that I shouldn't just yet.

After a nail-biting month wondering if I should get the boxes out again, Sinead called to tell me that her brother was coming to the rescue and would pay off the money past due. He was also going to cover most of the mortgage in the foreseeable future. I didn't want to believe it at first, but it was true.

Strangely, the stress that had hung over the house for so long started to take its toll on it, physically. Paint flaked, wood warped, the deck began to lean, and the roof began to leak. Every rainfall brought water into my little home, via the rotting windows. One day, I heard a loud crash, and I ran outside to find that a pane of glass from an upstairs window had simply fallen out. The house was dying—and yet I stayed put.

Then, six months after the foreclosure scare, I joined a local choir. And there he was, my chu-chi face, in the bass section. Like a moth to the flame I began to hover around him at every rehearsal, and before long we were inseparable. Soon after our relationship had begun, I retrieved the list from my sock drawer and read it again. Seeing just how many of the qualities on my list matched the man I had fallen in love with, I began to cry, as I realized that my search for The One was over. He didn't have the Scottish accent I had requested, but you can't have everything.

So, I did move out of that ramshackle house, and I now live in a lovely home in Montrose, California, with my wonderful husband, (who is a fantastic cook, by the way) our cat Gavroche, and our beautiful ten-month-old son, Elliott. While writing this story, I took the list out of my sock drawer and showed it to my husband for the first time. He smiled that chu-chi smile of his.

Divine Intervention

The dice of God is always loaded.
- Emerson

How many times have you heard, "God works in mysterious ways"? One of these ways is in miracles. Divine intervention is an astonishing event or a miracle believed to be caused by the active involvement of an unseen beneficent hand. Similar to grace—a gift freely given—Divine intervention cannot be planned for or controlled. It just happens, and it happens when we are most in need.

Angels in human form, a missed plane that saved our lives, a word from a stranger that shifts the outcome of a situation or simply our mood, these are all evidence of the Divine intervening in our lives. By acknowledging minor and major miracles we nurture a deep sense of connection and peace.

The Christmas Branch

By Sandra Maclean

It was late August 2005. I had moved into the house I had always dreamed of after years of apartment living. The first thing I thought to myself was, *I am going to have a real Christmas—a Christmas like I had not experienced since the passing of my mother in 2002.* I imagined having my whole family spend the weekend. It was my heart's wish to see us all together enjoying the loving holiday I grew up with and that I wanted, in turn, to give to my children.

Being out of work as Christmas approached, I did not know how I was going to pull off the big holiday I wanted to, but low and behold, I was hired by a department store and began working just ten days before Christmas. After our recent move, my home was cluttered with my twenty-five years of accumulated belongings, as well as the entire possessions of my mother-in-law who had left the house to my husband and me—double everything. She thought of me as her daughter, and I wanted to honor her memory in having the extended families together here under her roof. It would also be the first Christmas my husband was without his mother.

Getting the job was an affirmation for me. I had declared my intentions well in advance to my children and family. Now Christmas was ten days away and though I felt tired and most definitely not prepared, I put the word out to family.

Then I became sick with the flu. To add to this, I had a new litter of puppies, which meant seven dogs running around the house. Still, I was working and determined to have my "Mom's" traditional Christmas. My sister, Melody, called me four days before Christmas and asked, "Are you sure you are up to all of this?" I really had to consider it, so I said I would call her back. I was truly beginning to feel overwhelmed.

I started to pray to Spirit for an answer. I affirmed, "I just know I am guided to the right decision." I prayed all morning while at work and then I let it go. When break time came around, I decided to go to my car just to get some fresh air. Why I thought it would be restful to go to my car on the fifth floor of the parking structure, I have no clue. As I was walking up the wide, winding staircase, a man was walking right next to me. I don't know why, but I blurted out my problem to this seemingly friendly fellow.

I said to this total stranger that I have a real dilemma going on. He perked up and graciously said with interest, "How can I help?" So I told him the story of how I wanted a real Christmas this year, and my house was a mess and I was sick and I have all these puppies running around and I just started a new job and I was so exhausted, and how much I wanted to give this experience to my children. At that moment, we reached the fifth floor, and stopping, we made eye contact. I noticed he was rather pale and a bit sweaty around his hairline. I sensed he was not well. I shifted my attention to him.

"Are you okay?" I asked. He replied to me that I should have my "Mom's" Christmas, no matter what—that I could do it. Who cares about the mess, the puppies? It is about family, tradition, and most of all, it is about love. I was energized by his adamant conviction and knew he was right, even as I sensed something was not quite right with him.

The man was quiet for a second, looking at the ground. He then just blurted out that he was just diagnosed with terminal cancer and that he was only 37 years old. He was married with two small children and he was very angry. I was stunned and recognized that this was a very profound moment. It was a moment where two total strangers connected on a very deep level. I just listened as he told me the whole experience, from beginning to right where we were standing. He said he was at the

177

mall looking for a present for his wife. He had given me his total presence and had not trivialized what advice I was seeking. I did feel my concerns were rather trivial, regardless.

He confessed with stress he just couldn't think right now and asked me, please, for advice as to what he should buy his wife. I replied without hesitation, "Anything with diamonds." He chuckled and said, "Yes, of course, jewelry." He said that he was madly in love with his wife and she was madly in love with him. My heart was breaking.

As suddenly as we met, we had to part. I looked him in the eyes and wished him the best, and then we hugged and walked in separate directions. We never exchanged our names. I knew immediately it was a divine intervention that had put my whole life into perspective. On the way back to work I called my sister and said to her, "Christmas is on at my house; be there or be square. See you Christmas Eve."

Now the mad dash began. I had two days to pull this "miracle" together and I wasn't bothered at all, because I kept my staircase man in my heart and I felt centered.

First order of business was the Christmas tree. My husband called me at work the day before Christmas Eve and said, "There are no Christmas trees left on the whole planet; however there is this big pine branch, and the tree lot person said I could have it." "Take it," I said. "We will make it work."

When I arrived at home after a long evening shift and thousands of Christmas shoppers, I proceeded to work on getting the house in some sense of order. I stuck the Christmas branch into one of those outdoor clay fireplaces that is a decorative item in my house. It fit perfectly. Then I went to bed. The next day my husband did the food shopping. I did some gift shopping and worked until five p.m. on Christmas Eve.

My sister and my nephew arrived late; she took one look at the house and began to laugh. She was going with the flow and offered to run out and get Kentucky fried chicken for dinner. We all had an early night. The next morning all of the kids arrived early—five huge young men between 18 and 23 cramped in this small house with parents, aunts and uncles and dogs. I stuck the turkey in the oven and cranked on some Andy Williams and we all started to decorate the Christmas branch. When it was done we stood back to take a look. Everyone laughed in amazement and good humor and agreed it was indeed a beautiful branch. We proceeded to spend the morning opening gifts, drinking eggnog, and sharing our favorite Christmas memories, to my glorious delight. Soon the turkey began to give out an aroma that filled the house. If there is an aroma of Christmas, turkey is it!

After a sumptuous dinner with all hands on deck, the evening ended with playing group games, some good wine and a lot of laughs. It was loony tunes and it worked beautifully. I told the story to the boys about the man who inspired me. They were speechless in awe. I then blessed the gentleman and his family and gave thanks to God for the gift of our encounter. I will never forget him, nor will I ever forget the joyous and memorable Christmas that was given to each one of us that year because of him. I heard that if you let love go, it will show up everywhere. I find this to be true and the event that led to a family Christmas, precious in our memories, is my proof.

In the Twinkling of an Eye

By Arthur Barrett

It happened about 18 years ago. My daughter was about three or four years old at the time and I was taking her out for dinner. Her mother and I were newly separated and planning on getting divorced. I was just about making ends meet and I was not in a great place, emotionally or mentally. It was a terrible period in my life.

I found a nice place to eat that I thought my daughter would enjoy; it was brightly lit and colorful. We settled at a counter area in the middle of the restaurant to eat our meal. I looked around and really took in my environment. We faced the area where people came up to order so I could see people coming and going. I noticed a kind, middle-aged, conservatively dressed woman sitting near us, and she began to talk to me. She said what a delight it was to see a father out with his young daughter enjoying a meal.

As she said the words, I was flooded with a wonderful feeling and my mood was uplifted. Just then I was briefly distracted. I tended to my daughter and when I looked up, the lady was not there. I had not even had a chance to respond to her and was mystified as to where she had gone. I did not see her leave.

I got up and went to the door to see if I could catch her, but she was nowhere to be seen. I quickly moved through the restaurant to the back seating area, but no, she was not there either. Rejoining my daughter I watched the restroom door in case she had gone there. She did not come out. She seemed to have vanished into thin air.

It was so mystifying and I was so altered in my mental state by the encounter that I came to believe she was an angel. She lightened my load, made me feel a lot better, and I came away feeling I was headed in the right direction. What better reason to have an angel come visit?

Bridging the Gap

By Jon William Lopez

Back in the 1980's I was living in Brooklyn Heights, New York, in a ground level studio apartment in a four-story brownstone one block from the famous Promenade. Paved with brick and concrete block, this curving stretch above the Brooklyn Queens Expressway is lined with trees, park benches, playgrounds, flowerbeds and old street lamps. It offers a stunning view of the East River, the Statue of Liberty, lower Manhattan and the Brooklyn Bridge. Back then the World Trade Towers were still standing in all their magnificence. I would spend hours there, reclining on the benches with a cushion, listening to music on my portable cassette player, reading, or simply people-watching.

I was in my 30's and a freelance cartoon animator, making a fairly decent living working at small studios and production houses on commercials, educational films and half-hour animated TV specials. Back in 1976 I'd even co-directed an hour-long animated Bicentennial special for the local ABC network, for which I received an Emmy nomination. Being a freelancer, however, and in a business that was sporadic at best, work wasn't steady, and for the past several months I'd been unemployed. Money had grown very tight, and on this particular occasion I found myself nearly broke, with the rent due the very next day. I was overcome with fear, desperation and helplessness, and didn't know what I was going to do. I still had food in the fridge, but that was about it!

Sitting in my apartment was solving nothing, so I decided to take a walk. It was a warm early summer evening, the sun was still up, and the light was beginning to take on that golden glow. This was my favorite time of day. I walked rather aimlessly, not knowing where I was going, having no destination in mind. Out of habit, I found myself wandering towards the Promenade, where I'd spent many a comforting hour in contemplation, relaxation and meditation. I walked slowly along the one-third mile long stretch, only half-conscious of the breathtaking view, my mind overcome by my desperate situation.

As I reached the end of the Promenade, I focused on the majestic Brooklyn Bridge, which connects the boroughs of Manhattan and Brooklyn, spanning the East River. It was within walking distance, and without really knowing why, I felt myself being drawn towards it. Having traversed the bridge many times before, I recalled that there was a raised walkway along the centerline for pedestrians and cyclists, along which were also benches where you could sit and gaze out at the East River, with Brooklyn on the left and Manhattan on the right. I trudged along the walkway and chose a spot about halfway across, sitting on a bench facing west. The sun was setting and everything was bathed in a golden glow. The activity on the bridge, people walking or cycling by, traffic whooshing by below, the sounds of boats on the river and the distant bustle and hum of the city all blended and washed over me as so much white noise. In fact, because of the panicked state of mind I was in, I allowed it to blanket me in a kind of aural cocoon.

Despite being raised in an atheist household, I'd always had a fascination for metaphysics, the psychic realm and anomalous phenomena. I was just beginning to scratch the surface of spirituality. In college I learned Transcendental Meditation (TM), which I still practice to this day. Perhaps as a result of my upbringing, I didn't believe in a higher deity with volatile human characteristics that sat up in the sky and passed judgment on his lowly creations, but I wasn't sure what I believed in. I'd been reading about the technique of creative visualization and the concept that our thinking created our reality.

However, I still hadn't heard of what is termed "affirmative prayer," and that it could be used to transform my experience. A friend had recently introduced me to his Buddhist practice and the mantra "Nam(u) Myoho Renge Kyo" (pronounced nam-meh-oho-rengeh-kio). The purpose of chanting this mantra is to attain perfect and complete awakening, "Buddha wisdom," or enlightenment. Followers of Nichiren Buddhism consider the chant to represent the name of the ultimate law permeating the universe, and that humans are at one with it.

Although I wouldn't become familiar with this law until several years later, I nonetheless began chanting this mantra over and over silently in my mind, alternating it with my TM mantra. If an extraneous thought entered my mind, no matter what it was, I allowed it to come and go, and went back to repeating those mantras, having no rhyme or reason, no intention or goal. I simply surrendered to the process and the words. I eventually found myself in a state of complete and total peace, calm and serenity. Two hours went by, and when I finally made my way back home, it felt like I was floating. All stress and worry had vanished. I felt whole and complete. That night, I was able to sleep peacefully and soundly, knowing all was well. In that present moment, then and there, I recognized that I was safe, cared for and secure.

The very next day, the phone rang and I was offered a job. My dry spell of unemployment had broken. Coincidence? I may have thought that once, but knowing now that the Universe is intelligent and reflects back to me what I think into It, I realize that this was an incontrovertible demonstration of Divine Intervention and an overwhelming spiritual response to an urgent need. I am now a full-time student of New Thought spiritual principles and continue to use universal laws through affirmative prayer and other practices to create miracles in my life. As a licensed, professional prayer practitioner, I also offer these tools to others and empower them to do the same.

Do You Want to Live or Die?

By Amanda Sargenti

I remember this day as if it were last week. It was a Sunday early evening, pouring cats and dogs. Even though it was against my better judgment to drive on the 405 freeway under these conditions, I could not justify not visiting my friend for her birthday. After wishing her many blessed wishes, I decided to head back home again and not wait out the storm.

As I was driving on the heavily trafficked freeway, I began to contemplate my life. Even though I make it a habit to periodically assess everything in my life, this was different. Not that hopelessness and despair had become my best companions, but life had somehow snuck up on me, presenting many diverse challenges. Furthermore, the graduate school I was attending allowed me to enter an existential frame of mind. My daily ponderings consisted of questions such as, "What does it all mean? Does it even matter? I know things are challenging in my life at the moment and I do wear the perfume of a hint of depression quite well, but do I care to be alive? Isn't life a part of death and isn't death a part of life? Isn't it all one of the same continuum? Hmm, maybe I am tired of living...?"

My contemplative thoughts were suddenly interrupted by an ambulance. Although off duty, it rushed by me and began to swerve in and out of my lane, causing me to make some rapid decisions. Quickly, I accelerated my car to safety. Since "it never rains in California," I was not too familiar with the concept of hydroplaning. My reality had quickly changed from being in control to being out of control, as my car started to spin towards the left. Of course the rain had picked up and so I was fighting for visibility. Closing my eyes in a panic and attempting to regain my inner balance, I was clenching onto my steering wheel for dear life, while extending my legs and feet completely, allowing my car to accelerate in speed and the number of pirouettes it made.

"Disneyland? Am I riding the tea cups? I'm getting dizzy with all this spinning...But wait! Why am I feeling scared?" After striking the far left center divider I grew petrified, realizing I was still on the freeway. "Now what?" I thought to myself.

As if listening to my internal monologue, a gentle, deep, male voice asked me a question I will never forget: "Do you want to live or die?"

"Ah, must I decide now? Well, I guess I will go with live." I surprised myself with this sudden response, for I had felt ambivalence.

"Then, foot off gas!" I was instructed. "Turn wheel to the left!" was my second command.

Even though I obeyed, my car started to circle again, this time covering the next three right lanes. "Wait, maybe I am going to die here after all...What about seeing a nice bright light then? Isn't that what people see right before...Ok, so what is the big idea then?"

As I stared out of my front window trying to orient myself as to which direction I might be facing, I remember seeing a dull, endless shade of white. No cars, no landscape, no light, just an absence of anything and everything. "So, what are you trying to show me here, God?"

The same familiar voice explained something to me: "If you chose life, live it! Don't live half-assed! Your reality and life is your canvas! Paint it! Create! Be an active participant in your life!"

Humbled, I was trying to digest this reality check while at the same time checking myself back to the present and finding physical safety. Ashamed that I was so arrogant with my ambivalence about living and still spinning across the next two right lanes, my car somehow miraculously stopped; perpendicular to the right side divider.

With my eyes closed, and unsure if I was alive or dead, I began tapping my body to ensure I had all my limbs and was not bleeding. Although physically I seemed to be fine, I was unsure of what had just happened. Trying to discern if I was hearing voices in my head or I had been guided by a higher force, I soon became overwhelmed by an intense rush of love and warmth coming over me and covering my body like a blanket. Tears welled up in my eyes as I realized what had just occurred. I had been given a choice regarding my life, and a chance to snap out of my apathetic mind frame.

Before I could wholeheartedly give thanks to you know who, "Knock, knock! Hey lady, are you ok?" A gentle soul dressed in a highway patrol uniform was asking me some basic questions for his report. "Don't worry! I saw the whole thing! I was right behind you. I saw how the ambulance was entering..." I don't remember the rest. However, I do recall seeing the ambulance that had stopped and was pulled to the side. I also remember the traffic suddenly ceasing when my car was spinning out of control, as if an angel somehow stopped all the cars with its wing, preventing any crashes whatsoever. "Lady, you are very lucky! People like you don't walk out of here alive after pulling off what you just did!"

Well, people like me are blessed to have second chances as they are reminded to live fully and make their life count. I smiled to myself as I waited for the tow truck to pick me up.

Epilogue - Uhuru Peak

God Living sings to me in the soft tones of Swahili as we rest together under a crescent moon and the Southern Cross. He is patient with me. He tells me I must move at my own pace, drink lots of water, only lift my foot enough to glide over the ground: this will conserve energy. I am filled with doubts. But I have no headache, no symptoms, nothing to prevent me moving forward. I could stop and turn back but I can think of no good reason. My flashlight battery's run down so I move in the halo of light from God Living's. There is nothing to look at in the blackness but his feet moving before me and I stay close. I see light up ahead in the distance from the flashlights of other climbers. There are chunks of ice in my water bottle.

Five days into climbing Mount Kilimanjaro my companion, Tom, needs to quit. I have no idea how he will come to terms with this: the idea of not making it to the top, not finishing what he started? He can console himself, I suppose; he is in good company. Edmund Hillary had to be air-lifted off of this mountain because he tried to ascend too quickly. Altitude sickness can result in death from either fluid accumulation in the lungs or the swelling of the brain tissue. It has nothing to do with fitness or preparedness, and least of all, with commitment to the task.

I am just along for the adventure. When Tom, the driving force behind our expedition, has to give up, I think I will too. I am not attached to any part of this seven day enterprise in Africa. Being on this continent is a dream come true; I have no particular passion to conquer the mountain just because it's there.

In my moment of decision, I look up at the shining, white cap of Mount Kilimanjaro, or as the locals call it—Kibo, shading my eyes from the morning sun, now shining from behind its summit. I realize I am not done. I will go on.

A lone woman on a climb, there is a certain thrill to it. Of course I am not alone; I am guided by God Living. And I don't mean that in the sense of the Spirit within me, for at this time I have no language that I am comfortable with for a higher consciousness. My guide, in the form of a beautiful African man with the gentlest face, has the given Christian name of God Living.

I know there are no co-incidences. From the first day I was introduced to this man I knew I was in good hands. God Living exudes a peaceful and grounded energy and a quietly confident demeanor. As I watch Tom leave camp I think, *from here on, its God Living and me; how bad can that be!*

Leading me across dramatic landscapes of volcanic Africa this calm presence speaks little and moves slowly, closing his dark eyes before he answers the simplest question, giving thought to every subject put before him. I want to engage him more, to learn about his life and who he is, but what I learn from him is what he wants to teach me and what I assimilate as I follow silently in his footsteps.

Crossing barren expanses affording magnificent views, at times a yawing space opens up between us as my pace slows. I never lose sight of him on this Mars-like landscape; surreal at times, two lone people moving across the immense terrain, conscious of each other, stopping for water-breaks and continuing. It seems we are the only people on this stony planet. I wonder if I will make it to the top. I think of Tom and how he is doing. After hours of walking my mind tires of thinking and falls silent, I experience moments of pure presence to all my sensations and a deep tranquil pleasure in being alive.

I do not sleep a wink at Barafu hut, limited oxygen makes it impossible. I listen to the tent zipper jangling in the wind. At midnight God Living wakes me and tells me to wear every item of clothing I have. This will be the most difficult part of the climb. I wonder why I am doing this at all. This thought comes back to me many times as we hike almost vertically on loose shale, rattling and grating underfoot. I stop often. The repetitious footsteps in black nothingness leave me with only my thoughts. I think of the problems I left behind back home but they are not sufficient distraction. I think of Ireland and my family, their lives and my impending visit. I swing between being here, enjoying a night hike, forgetting about the goal and in the next moment wishing to be done with the mountain. Each time I rest I want to close my eyes and fall asleep. There is nothing to look at, everything is internal and my mind fights with my body even as it acquiesces to my intention to go on.

After six hours we reach the rim of the crater and there we are rewarded by the dawn breaking over the horizon and transforming the grey snowy landscape to a vivid amethyst and sapphire blue. *I did it* I think but there is no sense of elation or achievement then. I look around at the creamy azure snow filling the caldera and at the dark silhouettes of people moving in slow motion off to my left. I do not appreciate that this is a view that few see in this lifetime, all I can think is *now I can go down.*

I turn to God Living and he says no, I must go another half hour to the highest point, called Uhuru, Swahili word for Freedom. I will regret it if I do not he tells me. "At your pace," he says "You lead."

So I go and the wind sweeps around us getting inside the collar of my jacket as I pull out my camera from underneath my clothes. I'm afraid of frostbite. I quickly snap some pictures and put my camera away before it freezes. I try to appreciate all that I am experiencing but it is difficult to take it all in. On reaching the summit God Living kneels and I assume silently says a prayer. My hands are numb in my gloves.

The trip down takes two days and I get to see in daylight the landscape I traversed in the night. I anticipate with great excitement the prospect of a hot bath.

When we reach the ranger station at the base a small crowd of barefoot African shabbily dressed children watch, giggling and pointing, as I receive my certificate from the ranger. It is signed by God Living. I climb into the Land Rover that will take me to the hotel were Tom waits and I catch a glimpse of myself in the side mirror. I am shocked to see my face. I have been so immersed in being; in silent awareness of every sensation and every nuance of my environment I seem to have forgotten I am a separate entity.

It is time to say goodbye to God Living. I am emotional and do not want to let go of this shared experience. He shakes my hand firmly and his final words to me are "God be with you."

As the years have passed Kilimanjaro stands out in my memory as it does on the plains of Africa, as a shining high point. I realize today that I wanted to conquer the mountain more than I was aware back then, but it was not a physical mountain. As Edmund Hillary said himself, "It is not the mountain we conquer but ourselves." A summit equally daunting, if not more so, are the fears that have stood between me and my freedom. I have used the same tenacity and dogged determination to conquer what prevents me from being true to myself and doing what calls to me to do. I continue to work on conquering limits I have accepted for myself and to encourage others in their goals of doing the same. I do it at my own pace. I do it despite the world's readiness to nay-say, to encourage fear or hopelessness or tell me I can't. Love is the light I use to find my way if I ever feel it's absence as I get lost in my frustration, anger or hurt I remember there is a source of love whose halo I can walk in. Finding the most loving thought or action brings me into the flow of the living Spirit once more; I add my ounce of love rather than something less healing to the world.

This book took on a life of its own once I believed in the idea. It was not my idea, just as the trip to Africa was not; it was something I went along with for the adventure and something that brought me unexpected joys and rewards. It has been my great pleasure to bring these inspirational people to you and I hope the sharing of their stories inspires you to write your own. In many cases the contributors felt a catharsis or healing from the process of looking objectively at their own journeys. Remember your story could inspire someone to go beyond their limits, to step beyond a comfort zone that is past its due date and go find the fresh experience that gives their life greater meaning. We are all on this path together; let's support each other in remembering our true nature as infinite love, as the Living Spirit itself, as God Living.

Namaste.
Joan Doyle

A Prayer for You

I offer this prayer for all those in need of peace today. I suggest that you read the prayer out loud. Hearing yourself speak these healing words has great power.

There is One Source of all that is. From this Source was created all that is seen and unseen, from the beginning to the end of time. I know the qualities of this Living Spirit to be infinite and ever present. They are goodness, joy, abundance, vitality, peace and expansiveness.

This Living Spirit is my life now. It is the life of all beings. No one is excluded.

I surrender to this infinite fountain of love and calm serenity, it is my security within. In the flow of this Living Spirit I allow it to do through me all that needs to be done by me. I am here by divine appointment and my life has purpose. It is my purpose to be an expression of the joy, love and wisdom of Spirit. This Living Spirit cannot be limited by the appearances of lack, fear, age, sickness or failure. I am the Spiritual Light that cannot fail. I am peace.

I give thanks for this changeless Truth and for the many blessings in my life.

I am grateful.

I now release this powerful word of Spirit and let it be.
And so it is,
Amen.

The Ten Core Concepts
of Centers for Spiritual Living

Known also as Religious Science or the philosophy of Science of Mind this movement was founded by **Ernest Holmes** (January 21, 1887 – April 7, 1960) an American spiritual writer, teacher, and leader.

1. **Oneness** - The Living Spirit or God is the Source of all that is. Everything in the manifest universe is made of this substance and is a unique, individualized expression of it.
2. **Triune Nature** - The Living Spirit expresses Itself in three aspects—Spirit or Oversoul, Soul, and Body. Each human being also has these same three aspects. Thus, there is God as macrocosm, human beings as microcosm.
3. **Creative Nature** - The Living Spirit thinks, and the world comes into being. Likewise, all human accomplishments originate in thought. Our human thinking process is a reflection of the Divine Creative Process in microcosm.
4. **Prayer** - All Good is eternally available to all who feel this indwelling Presence and is ready to flow into human experience. We activate this flow by means of acceptance, human faith and belief as well as prayer. Through affirmative prayer we align with Spiritual Truth and Universal Harmony that always exists.
5. **Wholeness** - Spirit is a transcendent, perfect whole that contains and embraces all seeming opposites. As human beings, we have free will and can choose what we experience, whether it be positive or negative. The same Principle that brings us freedom, prosperity, and joy also allows us to experience bondage, lack, or misery, according to our consciousness.

6. **Abundance** - All that anyone will ever need or desire is already provided by Universal Abundance. This applies to everybody, not just some people. Every person is heir to the riches of creation, without regard to merit.
7. **The Reciprocal Universe** - For every visible form there is an invisible counterpart. This means that what we receive corresponds to what we imagine and believe we can receive, the Law of Mental Equivalents. This also is the Golden Rule: that what we do to others will be done also to us.
8. **Forgiveness** - Human forgiveness is the process that frees us to live in the Eternal Now. It is the essential step before real spiritual growth can flourish. Science of Mind teaches that the ultimate goal of life is complete emancipation from all discord of every nature, and that this goal is sure to be attained by all.
9. **Immortality** - The Universal Truth about life is that life never ends. What we call death is simply the changing of one form of life for another. Death, the belief and perception that life must come to an end, is a human concept. As in birth the invisible becomes visible, so in dying the visible again becomes invisible. Life continues on another plane when the body has outlived its usefulness.
10. **The Christ** - The Christ is not a person, but a Principle, a Universal Presence, a state of consciousness that is present in all creation, within every person. Each human individual partakes of the Christ consciousness to the degree that he or she recognizes the Living Spirit within and lives out of that revelation of Truth. Jesus of Nazareth was a human individual who revealed awakened consciousness to the highest degree.

Derived from the Core Concepts of Science of Mind by
Dr. Ernest Holmes.
Copyright 2012 Centers for Spiritual Living

About The Editor/Author
Joan Doyle

Joan Doyle was born in Carlow, Ireland and worked in Tralee, Kinsale and Dublin until she was thirty. She has lived with a foot in two countries endeavoring to enjoy the best of both divergent worlds since her move to Los Angeles in 1993. An artist and an observer of the world around her she has enjoyed world travel, a successful career in art and a deepening purpose as a Spiritual Counselor. Life is an ever expanding adventure which she shares with her husband Justin, their dog Otis and cat Rosie. She tries to remember that every day is a gift.
Learn more about her counseling work
www.SpiritIsTalkingToYou.com
See her beautiful watercolors at www.theHouseArtist.com

If you have enjoyed this book and you have a Spirit story of your own you are invited to submit your story for publication via the website **www.SpiritIsTalkingToYou.com**

About the Contributors

Amanda Sargenti was born and raised in multicultural Switzerland by ethnically diverse parents. While being exposed to different countries, Amanda began using color, form and words at an early age to explore her inner and outer realities. After immigrating to California at age 16, Amanda obtained her B.A. in Speech and Communication and her M.A. in Clinical Art Therapy/Marriage, Family and Child Therapy. Her focus is to balance her painting and writing with working as a clinician and walking her spiritual path. Currently she is creating a workbook for individuals who are unsure of their life's journey.

Amy Lloyd has a bad case of creative overdrive spending her halcyon days acting, writing, painting and participation in general mischief. If it can be sung, painted or written – it will – is her motto. She has authored two young adult novels; *The Secret Lives of Freaks* and more recently *Molly Day*. Her writing has been published on hellogrief.org, L.A. Family magazine, Raw magazine and she has won the Naomi Rose "Writing from the deeper self" contest. She also authored and designed a photography book, *The Refrigerator Project*. Her written work has also been performed at Bang Theatre in Los Angeles. www.AmyLloydonline.com

Arthur Barrett, lives a full and varied life based in Montrose, California. From an early age he had an 'awakening' when he 'knew' all the Great Teachers were One. They come to cultures in their own time with a truth that was spoken so it could be understood. Soon after-wards he felt his third eye awoke. After many years of seeking he now knows a Peace and Joy that continues to expand and deepen. The angel story in this book is one of many dialogs that God has gifted him to show that love and support are always near.

Barbara Schiffman, C.Ht., ARCT, is a Life&Soul Coach, Hypnotherapist and Advanced Akashic Records Healing Practitioner and Certified Teacher (affiliated with Linda Howe's Center for Akashic Studies). She leads Akashic Healing workshops and Practitioner Certification trainings, and also does Akashic Readings by phone or in person. Barbara's articles on life balance and personal evolution have been published in Vision Magazine and anthology books including "Happiness Awaits You" and "2012: Creating Your Own Shift." She also authored and published "Living in Balance for Boomers" and "The Akashic Muse: Collaborating With Your Soul for Writing and Other Creative Endeavors" as books and ebooks.

Carrie McConkey-Herrera is a licensed and certified Spiritual Counselor and Virtues Facilitator and the creator and owner of Hoops & Virtues Basketball Programs. Her greatest blessing is the life she shares with her husband Efren Herrera and her 7 year old son Diego, in Granada Hills, California. Carrie is currently working on her first book entitled "The Gift of Motherhood" which is a divinely guided book about parenting. "My life started the day my son was born. I was given a gift and a divine understanding of parenting and now I share my gift with the world." www.hoopsandvirtues.com

Christy Shelton is a teaching artist and spiritual counselor living in Los Angeles. Although born in Hollywood California, she spent her formative years in Eugene, Oregon. The lush tapestry of trees that blanket the surrounding mountains, and deep experiences walking in the woods awakened her intuitive connection with the Holy Spirit in Nature. In addition, at her grandmother's promptings, she attended Catholic Sunday school in Eugene that called forth a Divine pattern within her to listen to and be guided by "God" – by Love. Her faith is made whole and maintained by the Creative Spirit moving through all things.

Chrystine Julian is the author of 10 books/ebooks. She has been an executive, a standup comic, minister, mystic, medium, musician, recording artist, spiritual healer/teacher, workshop leader, drum circle facilitator and poet. She has shared her various skills from North Carolina to Southern California and many locations in between. Information is available at ChrystineJulian.com

Dean Regan R.Sc.P. is a licensed practitioner with the Centers for Spiritual Living and core member of North Hollywood Church of Religious Science. He is a concert and recording artist, actor, singer and coach hailing from Chicago. His first love has always been theater which inspires him in his ministry: Spirit

Song. He performs solo concerts off Broadway and Standard music at performing arts centers nationally and sings as soloist at churches throughout Southern California. Dean has performed on and off Broadway, regional theatre, both television and film. His CD, "Give My Regards to Broadway" is available on iTunes. www.DeanRegan.com

Dearbhla Egan was born in 1964 in Carlow, Ireland. She lives with her husband, her five year old daughter and three dogs. She worked for many years as a Speech and Creative Drama teacher until she adopted her daughter in Vietnam. Through her unique life experiences and personal challenges she has learned a great deal about herself and others and now knows that tolerance and acceptance of the differences that ultimately bind us together are the greatest attributes we can have in order to live a life worth living.

Gertrude Anne Doyle B.A. H.D.E. is a professional artist (aka Trudi Doyle.) Her work is inspired by the beauty of the everyday and by a sense of reverence for the natural world and mythology which surrounds it. Her paintings have been used on book covers and as illustrations and have been commissioned by many public bodies including the Irish Department of Education. Her work is collected throughout the world. In 1999 she established her school "Bunbury Art Studio" in Ireland providing art workshops for adults throughout the summer each year. She also tutors art in Italy and France.
http://www.trudi-doyle.artistwebsite.com
http://www.etsy.com/shop/ARTbyTRUDI
http://www.trudidoyle.blogspot.com

Jon William Lopez, RScP, was born in San Juan, Puerto Rico. He is a former cartoon animator and has worked at Disney, Dreamworks, and for 3 seasons on "The Simpsons". Always interested in metaphysics, after moving to L.A. in 1990 he began his true spiritual path by becoming a student of New Thought and the Science of Mind teaching. He is now a licensed spiritual prayer practitioner and author of "Perfect Praying: 5 Simple Steps That Make Prayers Work." He is at work on his second book. His websites are www.jonwilliamlopez.com and www.perfectprayerpractitioner.com.

Joseph Doyle is a graduate of The Irish Institute of Photography. Living close to nature in the Irish countryside, his fondness for animals and the great out-doors, inspires him to use his camera to freeze moments in time, capturing our environment's wondrous beauty and splendor. If he is not taking photographs he will be found fishing near Rathdrum, County Wicklow. http://joseph-doyle.artistwebsites.com/index.html

Julie Penman Livesey was born in England, she gained her appreciation of beauty, both natural and hand-crafted, from the picturesque landscape and quaint architecture of her home county. Her love of art and the movies took her to college to learn Animation, Video and Photography. For the last 22 years she has worked on many animated projects in both England and the U.S. Books are also a passion for Julie, who loves to rummage in thrift stores for First Editions to add to her collection. She lives in Los Angeles, California, with her husband and young son Elliott – her new photographic muse.

Justin Elledge is a true renaissance man - inventor, entrepreneur, vocational nurse, nutrition consultant, radio personality and perhaps his greatest gift of all, that of Medical Intuition; a gift he was blessed with on his lifelong path to healing the self. Going where few would tread to find the truth his path to health and service to others has led him through a series of health challenges including migraine headaches, heavy metal poisoning, and malabsorption syndrome. He has survived and thrived while continuing

to seek answers to help his worldwide clients.
www.viewmyhealth.com
www.wonderweignt.com

Kristina Keefer is a Senior Manager in Human Resources at ABC-CLIO in Santa Barbara, California. She studied Organizational Psychology at Antioch University and is originally from Los Angeles California.

Laurie St. Clare an Evolutionary Astrologer, Intuitive Counselor and Healer, has been passionate about astrology and metaphysics since childhood. At the age of 10 experiencing the death of her oldest brother plunged her deep into the mysteries of life. A native of Los Angeles she enjoys the wide variety of culture, religion and sunshine there. Her greatest pleasure is inspiring people to make the best possible choices for themselves and live "the Sweet Life." www.SweetLifeAstrology.com

Mary Hylan, is happy to be a counselor and professional singer. She is a people-person who loves to inspire and empower others. For ten years she has been an active, licensed Religious Science Practitioner (RScP), or spiritual counselor, as well as holding a license as a Marriage and Family Therapist (LMFT). Her prayer counseling ministry brings her great joy. She has a Grammy Award for her jazz work, has created her own Christmas CD, and has sung for countless live performances and recording sessions, including many major films. Mary endeavors to see God/Good in everyone and everything! marhylc@aol.com

Robert Duffy whilst he was a designer and fabricator of farm buildings in his day job, has been writing articles and stories for several years. In his fiction he is quite adept at capturing the drama that can lurk beneath the simplest of events or obser-vations. His books include "Jack in the Box" (short stories) and "One Hundred Years Too Soon" about his area's involvement in the 1798 rebellion. He is married to Audrey and they have three children and two grandchildren. He lives in Hacketstown, Carlow, Ireland; (the postman knows him.) Robert can also be contacted at robtduffy@gmail.com

S. Kay, 73, formerly of Hollywood, California, is a mother of five, retired Advertising Executive, Business Owner and Sales Executive. Currently she is a Science of Mind Practitioner.

Sabrina Johnson is a Practitioner with North Hollywood Church of Religious Science. She combines her spiritual studies with her love of literature when she writes about books that she has read from a metaphysical point of view. The name of her blog, literalperfection.com, reflects how she sees so much of life when she sees from the side of Spirit – that is, life is unfolding and revealing itself perfectly.

Sandi Duncan is an intuitive healer and has a holistic healthcare practice in La Crescenta, California. In 2006 Sandi was diagnosed with advanced ovarian cancer and given a poor prognosis for survival. Drawing upon her years of spiritual practice and using energy healing techniques, drumming and meditation as well as traditional western medicine, Sandi defied the prognosis and has been in remission for over 6 years. She has made it her mission to help others in providing tools for managing "wellness." Sandi's mantra is "All is Well" and it has helped her face many of life's challenges. www.StressSoulutions.com

Sandra Maclean was born and raised in Los Angeles, California and began her life as an artist at the age of two when she cut up her mother's dress and made a doll out of it. Constantly creating she enjoys many forms of art, including painting and writing. A mother to two grown sons, she is a licensed Spiritual Counselor with North Hollywood Center for Spiritual Living where she enjoys being of service. Life is always interesting and fulfilling as she aspires to live by the words - If you live life in the flow of new beginnings you will be okay.

Sandra Phillips is a business mentor, psychic, writer and artist. Combining 15 years corporate business experience with her unique gift of perception she offers clear information that can be used by individuals as they navigate their way through their career or life. Her first book 'A Journey into the Light' is a biographical account of her life. She is also a public speaker in areas of her expertise, writing, painting, business intuition & development, psychic ability, healing and energy. Her website is www.soulaffinity.com

Sean Kelly In 1995 Sean, musician, writer, inspirational speaker, founded Mind Matters to teach people to use more of their mind's potential. In 2000, after the death of his father, Sean began to develop his own talent for music. He plays classical guitar, the pipes, sings barbershop as well as in two choirs. His first album "Dare to Dream" was released in 2005. He believes that everything we experience in life offers us a lesson to help us realize the truth about ourselves. Raised in Dublin, Ireland, he received a Science Degree in Physics and Mathematics from Trinity College. www.SeanMKelly.com

Tom Rebold After studying engineering at MIT, Tom Rebold spent 13 years working on NASA's Deep Space Network for the Voyager through Mars Pathfinder missions. Since 2000, he has been teaching engineering and computer science at Monterey Peninsula College. Some highlights of his non-professional work include performing in a theatrical production at McMurdo Station, Antarctica; seeking Mayan ruins from satellite images on the ground in Yucatan; and writing software to detect patterns in whale/human musical interactions. Recently his kinetic sculpture, "Longing for North" was shown at ArtArk in San Jose. Examples of this and other artworks of his can be viewed at http://tomrebold.com/art